"This is a thoughtful, inspiring, and practical guide to how to use compassion to better our lives, communities, and world. Weaving cutting-edge scientific discoveries with their own personal experiences as world-renowned scientists and practitioners, Professors Guerra and Williams challenge us to rediscover our own shared humanity through connecting more deeply with ourselves and others."

Paul Piff, PhD, *associate professor of psychological science, University of California, Irvine*

"If you want more joy, peace, and meaning in your life and relationships, this book is a must read. As a student in Professor Guerra's compassion courses, I have experienced first hand how the lessons in this book are life changing. When I was facing extreme personal stress—full-time student, working odd jobs, and dealing with a stage 3 cancer diagnosis—the lessons I learned in the compassion courses contributed profoundly to helping me manage and be at peace with these challenges, and I carry them with me wherever I go. I hope you will do the same, and that together we can navigate life's challenges and create a more compassionate world."

Daelyn Nicole Daniloff, BA, *University of California, Irvine*

"In a time of cruel international wars and profound polarization in many countries, where dehumanization of the adversary allows violence, war crimes, and grave human rights abuses, Nancy Guerra and Kirk R. Williams offer us hope and optimism. Guerra and Williams teach us to practice empathy and compassion in our everyday life and operationalize the idea of 'love thy neighbor'. They also provide us with a guide on how to teach compassion to our students, our families, and our coworkers. This book is a very useful resource for any workplace and any family."

Martin Burt, PhD, *founder and CEO of Fundación Paraguaya and Poverty Stoplight; former mayor of Asunción, Paraguay*

The Seven Virtues of Highly Compassionate People

What are the practical implications of truly caring about yourself and others, of approaching each day with an open mind, an open heart, and a desire to reduce the suffering of all living beings? Can we learn compassion as a way of life, as an antidote to violence and cruelty? In *The Seven Virtues of Highly Compassionate People*, social scientists Nancy Guerra and Kirk R. Williams provide easy-to-follow steps to help you understand the *what*, the *why*, and the *how* of compassion. They bring together cutting-edge research, inspiring spiritual teachings, and their own life experiences to help you bring compassion front and center in your life. Not only is compassion good for you and those around you, but it is the key to a more peaceful and just world.

Nancy Guerra holds a doctorate in human development and psychology from Harvard University. She has designed and implemented interventions to promote social-emotional learning and prevent violence with children and youth.

Kirk R. Williams has a PhD in sociology from the University of Arizona. He is professor emeritus in the Department of Criminology, Law and Society at the University of California, Irvine. He studies the causes and prevention of youth violence and adult intimate partner violence with an emphasis on domestic violence risk assessment.

The Seven Virtues of Highly Compassionate People

Tools for Cultivating a Life of Harmony and Joy

Nancy Guerra and Kirk R. Williams

Routledge
Taylor & Francis Group
NEW YORK AND LONDON

We are immensely grateful to Kelly and Jim Hallman and the board of directors of The Living Peace Foundation. With their generous support, they have made this book and all of our work on compassion possible.

CONTENTS

ABOUT THE AUTHORS

Nancy Guerra is a developmental psychologist, Professor Emeritus of Psychological Science, and former Dean of the School of Social Ecology at the University of California at Irvine. Her research has focused on understanding and preventing problem behaviors among children and youth, and promoting positive development and well-being. She has worked extensively with schools, families, community groups, service providers, and national and international agencies across a range of prevention and development efforts. Her work is based on cognitive-behavioral processes, emphasizing the role of thoughts and beliefs in determining and modifying behavior and how these are shaped by context.

Professor Guerra has received over $30 million in federal and private grant funding. She has been involved in the development and evaluation of several large-scale prevention programs including serving as principal investigator for the Metropolitan Area Child Study, an eight-year development and prevention study with urban and inner-city children in Chicago, funded by NIMH; a district-wide SAMHSA-funded Safe Students project in Southern California to promote healthy development and prevent risk through Wellness Centers; and a CDC-funded Academic Center of Excellence on Youth Violence Prevention. She is a former Associate Editor at *Child Development* and former Editor at the *Journal of Research on Adolescence*. She has also served in leadership roles on a broad range of national and international task forces and initiatives to promote youth well-being, including *Know Violence: A Global Learning Initiative to Prevent Violence in Childhood*, a partnership with many different institutions including the Public Health Foundation of India, Harvard University, University of Cape Town, University of the West Indies, and London School of Hygiene and Tropical Medicine.

Kirk R. Williams is Professor Emeritus in the Department of Criminology, Law & Society at the University of California at Irvine (UCI). He previously served as Faculty Director of the UCI School of Social Ecology's interdisciplinary Ph.D. Core Program.

Throughout his career, he conducted research focusing on the understanding and prevention of violence. The research included studies of homicide rate variation across US cities, ranging from youth homicide and intimate partner homicide to homicide over stages of the life course. He also participated in a national survey of family violence, examining the role of legal sanctions in reducing non-fatal forms of intimate partner violence. He administered surveys of bullying in Colorado schools, with the aim of reducing bullying beliefs and behaviors. He also conducted studies in Colorado and Jamaica on youth firearm and gang violence.

Most of this violence research was conducted while affiliated with interdisciplinary research centers, including the Family Research Laboratory (FRL, Faculty Fellow) at the University of New Hampshire, the Center for the Study and Prevention of Violence (CSPV, Founding Associate Director) at the University of Colorado at Boulder, the Presley Center for Crime and Justice Studies (Presley Center, Co-Director), and the Southern California Academic Center of Excellence in Youth Violence Prevention (ACE-UCR, Co-Director), both at the University of California at Riverside. He was previously the Chair of the Department of Sociology and Criminal Justice at the University of Delaware.

He authored or co-authored over 90 peer-reviewed journal articles, book chapters, and technical reports on the causes and prevention of violence. He also co-edited a book on violence in schools. He received over USD10 million in grants from federal and state funding sources, in addition to private foundations. He still works with community-based groups and criminal justice agencies in violence prevention planning, implementation, and evaluation, with a special focus on domestic violence risk assessment.

PROLOGUE

Our guess is that if you are reading this book, you already believe in the power of compassion. We certainly do. But although we all have the capacity to act with compassion, it takes more than just belief or desire to bring it front and center in our lives. It takes knowledge, skills, and commitment to action.

As we note throughout this book, pain and suffering are inevitable, but how we respond to both is in our own hands. It is within our power to choose a course of action and create our path forward. Living a life filled with compassion is not a destination but an orientation to living, a

The Monon Biking and Pedestrian Trail, which runs 26 miles from Sheridan to Indianapolis, Indiana. A beautiful journey any time of the year.
Source: © Nancy Guerra and Kirk R. Williams

perspective toward life, a connection with your heart, and a journey that requires disciplined, daily practice. It is a journey we hope to share with you.

So, let's start with a simple question: What does it mean to be compassionate? When we ask people from different walks of life, we hear different answers. Here are some of the things people say:

- Compassion is being kind and caring.
- Compassion is all about empathy.
- Compassion is being mindful and grateful.
- Compassion is the desire to make the world a better place.
- Compassion is connection and valuing yourself and others.
- Compassion is appreciating what you have and helping others.

What comes to mind when you think about compassion? Is it empathy? Or being grateful? What about kindness? The truth is that compassion consists of many admirable virtues, including kindness and empathy, that are interconnected. In this book we highlight seven virtues linked to compassion and discuss how they can help you cultivate a life of harmony and joy. They are:

- Mindfulness
- Self-awareness
- Gratitude
- Perspective taking
- Empathy
- Kindness
- Altruism

Each of these virtues leads us to do good in the world, to develop kind and caring relationships with others, to respect ourselves, to act collaboratively, to be productive members of society, and to respect our planet Earth. Taken together, they provide a foundation not only for doing good but for preventing harm in any way we can, for preventing suffering in our own lives and the lives of others.

Indeed, compassion focuses on the prevention or alleviation of suffering. The word "compassion" comes from the Latin *pati* and the prefix *com*. The literal translation of *pati* is "to suffer" and the prefix *com* means "with." Following the Latin roots, the most common definitions of compassion include reference to a ***concern for the suffering or unmet need of self and others along with a desire to prevent or alleviate that suffering***.

In our own thinking about compassion, we highlight the importance of wanting to prevent and alleviate suffering, but we also
believe it is important to move beyond desire to action. In other
words, while compassion represents both a concern for and desire
to alleviate suffering, it also involves **taking action** in the face of
suffering however, whenever, and wherever possible. *Compassion
involves daily practice, and that practice is grounded in the idea of
our shared humanity.*

We often focus on how we differ from others and what divides us
either as individuals or based on the groups we belong to. But the truth
is, we have many more commonalities than differences. We all need and
want many of the same things, for example, food, shelter, safety, good
health, recognition, companionship, love, and purpose come to mind.
And we all suffer when these needs are not met. As the 14th Dalai Lama
has said:

> Whether we like it or not, we have all been born into this world
> as part of one great human family. Rich or poor, educated or un-
> educated, belonging to one nation or another, to one religion or
> another, adhering to this ideology or that, ultimately each of us
> is just a human being like everyone else. We all desire happiness
> and do not want suffering.[1]

Every single person on this planet has good days and bad days, successes
and failures. Have you ever read about someone rich and famous and
wondered how they could ever be sad, upset, or unhappy? As Brene
Brown discusses in her bestselling book, *Atlas of the Heart*, compassion
is part of what makes us human, a practice based on both the beauty and
pain of our shared humanity. [2]

What does the term *shared humanity* mean to you? Try to think
about or write down a few sentences that reflect your understanding and
appreciation of our common humanity. In the picture below, the students
came from diverse and often challenging backgrounds, and yet we all
experienced the awe and wonder of this 15th-century Incan citadel in

Kirk and Nancy at Machu Picchu where we took 10 students participating in the Global Service Scholars Program, funded by The Living Peace Foundation.
Source: © Nancy Guerra and Kirk R. Williams

much the same manner. We all shared in the experience of being part of a rich and diverse past and of living with hope and anticipation for the future. We all felt what it means to be human.

Speaking of awe and wonder, think about the last time you wandered through the forest, sat and listened to the ocean, stood in a magnificent building, or simply observed a beautiful flower. All these experiences help us get outside of ourselves and realize that there is something bigger that unites us in our common humanity. For some people, religion or a belief in a higher being brings this awareness to mind. The Japanese have a word for this profound sense of the beauty and mystery of the universe, a word that is simply too deep to be defined: *yugen*. Can you think of a time you have experienced *yugen*?

Compassion is not a new concept. It is common across major philosophical and religious traditions, a cornerstone of civil society, and the social glue that helps us coexist. Scientific research across diverse fields shows how the capacity for compassion is written on our biological birth certificate and revealed in the inner workings of our brain. Yet, although history is full of examples of compassion, it also is filled with too many instances of widespread and near-unimaginable suffering.

But suffering is part of life. As long as we live in this world, we will encounter difficult situations, and some of us will face more hardship than others. In some cases, adversity is beyond our control, for example, with natural disasters. In other cases, humans cause suffering for ourselves and others through destructive emotions like anger, hatred, and greed,

A beautiful lake we love to go to in the fall. Looking at the reflection of the golden aspens on the lake is to experience *yugen* and a deep sense of awe.
Source: © Nancy Guerra and Kirk R. Williams

or through destructive behaviors like aggression, violence, and war. And now, as the world becomes increasingly interconnected, our suffering becomes increasingly intertwined. A refugee crisis in one region creates a global crisis for resettlement; environmental pollution transcends geographic border; and the spread of a novel coronavirus cascades into a worldwide tragedy of human loss and suffering.

If humans have the capacity for compassion, what keeps it from being front and center in our lives? Haven't we often looked the other way, blamed the victim, or simply felt powerless to respond in a meaningful way? Sometimes we drown our self-criticism or self-pity in alcohol or sleepless nights. Or we "check the box" by volunteering for a few hours or giving a small handout to someone in need. But in all these instances, we fail to truly embrace compassion as a driving force in our lives. We often help those we like or those closest to us but shun those beyond our inner circle. Worse, we unintentionally or intentionally cause suffering for ourselves and others.

How do you react to suffering? Think about how you *perceive* the world around you, what you pay attention to, and what you either look away from or discount as irrelevant. When you walk by a homeless person asking for help on the street, do you talk to them, help them, or walk away? What about when the suffering goes beyond an individual? For example, when you read or hear about suffering caused by systemic racism, do you shrug your shoulders helplessly or consider ways to help? Or when *you* experience suffering, do you writhe in self-absorption and pain or try to turn your suffering into an opportunity to grow and learn from hard times? One of the greatest ironies of parenting is that when we try to protect our children from pain and suffering (as most parents always try to do), we also take from them opportunities to learn how to overcome adversity and build resilience.

Your thoughts also come into play. Do you remember a time when someone did something you didn't like and you immediately assumed they were trying to hurt you or being inconsiderate? What happened next? Did you find out more information or try to let the situation go? Or did your thoughts immediately lead to anger? It may be that you simply misunderstood the situation, failing to take the perspective of the other person. Or, unable to monitor your hostile thoughts, you let those thoughts spark negative emotions, unintentionally creating suffering for you (and likely for the other person).

Simply being aware of what interferes with compassion is an important first step, whether that means looking the other way or misinterpreting the actions of a friend. Of equal importance is learning how to embrace compassion, how to live a life guided by compassion in the broadest sense, and how you can contribute to making the world a better place in your own unique way.

> Although compassion directs our attention towards alleviating suffering, the seven virtues help us be more compassionate. In turn, compassion helps us promote well-being for ourselves, others both near and far, and the planet we live on. It helps us bring harmony and joy into our lives and the lives of others.

Let's pause for a moment to think about what it means to experience harmony and joy in our lives. From the beginning of life, not only do we want to avoid suffering but we want to live in harmony with others and experience joy.

The importance of living a harmonious life, of being at peace with ourselves and others, is emphasized across all major religions. Harmony creates a sense of balance and flow, a smooth functioning and connectedness between all living things. The Buddha spoke frequently about the need and value of harmony. Unity is a common theme in the Bible: "then make my joy complete by being like-minded, having the same love, being one in spirit and of one mind" (Philippians 2.2). Islam places great importance on unity and harmony, on treating all human beings with dignity and respect. Think about times in your life when you had contentious relationships with others? How did that make you feel? Now think about times when things seemed to flow effortlessly, much like a beautiful symphony. How did that make you feel?

Now let's think about the meaning of joy. Is it momentary pleasure? Extreme happiness? On the one hand, we believe that joy comes from being in the moment, being mindful of the wonders around us. Little children always remind us of this momentary joy. Just watch them jump up and down when it starts to snow or smile from ear to ear when they get cake and ice cream.

But we also experience a more enduring type of joy from somewhere deep in our soul. It has a wide wingspan, including a host of feelings such as delight, pleasure, wonder, and ecstasy. In *The Book of Joy: Lasting Happiness in a Changing World*, Archbishop Desmond Tutu talks about joy as a feeling much bigger and more enduring than happiness. To Tutu, joy is not dependent on getting what you want or other momentary pleasures. Joy is born out of the same understanding as compassion, specifically, the recognition that we are all connected to each other and to the universe.[3]

The momentary joy a 6-year-old feels with a giant ice cream cone. Children often remind us that joy is part of our essential nature. It is something we can all experience.
Source: © Nancy Guerra and Kirk R. Williams

Harmony, joy, and compassion share the capacity to become a way of living, a positive and engaged orientation to the world, not just a temporary feeling. They are clearly intertwined. **Living a compassion-driven life allows you to be in harmony with others, a positive orientation to living that also brings more joy. In turn, harmony and joy make you more compassionate.**

Now, think for a moment about how different our world would be if more people committed to being compassionate. What would happen if we extended compassion to those around us? This means that our perceptions, emotions, thoughts, and actions would be guided by our desire and our efforts to prevent or alleviate suffering. Extending compassion to those around us would also promote well-being, happiness, and joy for ourselves, our friends and family, people we don't even know, and ultimately the planet.

In this book, our approach to promoting compassion as a way of living cuts across many ways of thinking about and studying our world. We interconnect social and behavioral science research with writings from humanistic fields such as history, philosophy, religion, spirituality, and others. We also seek to link research and writings from these fields to our own personal experiences. We want to begin by sharing what each of us brings to writing this book and what inspired us to write it together. This includes our perspective on the status of things in the world today and, equally important, a recap of some of our own life experiences in both personal and professional regards. We took on the task

Kirk and Nancy taking a moment to relax.
Source: © Nancy Guerra and Kirk R. Williams

of writing this book not only as colleagues in the work we do but as soulmates and partners in life. We start by each telling our own story.

Kirk's Story

I've had my fair share of ups, downs, and mundane experiences like anybody else. But in reflecting on my life, I choose to dwell on experiences of wonder. When I say "wonder," I mean the emotional life experiences that give you goose bumps and elevate you to a place outside yourself. Those transcendent moments when "you" dissolve, become a part of everything around you and experience pure joy. Let me give you some examples drawn from deep memories.

As a child, I was blessed with loving and nurturing caregivers, especially caregiving women. I was particularly close to my maternal grandmother. Her name was Jennie, my mother's name was Jennie, and now my daughter's name is Jennie. I suppose that says something about her legacy.

My grandmother was a gift, an incredibly loving person. Many of my sensitive and empathic qualities are the result of our regular conversations in my early years. She would warmly hold both of my hands and look into my soul with her beautiful and penetrating blue eyes. Although she regularly offered wise counsel, one of the things she said frequently was: "Listen to the voice within you."

My maternal grandparents lived on a lake outside of Kansas City, Missouri in a rustic house named Belhaven. It was surrounded by a forest with limestone outcroppings, a barnyard, and an apple orchard. I recall wandering as a young child through the forest and into the orchard, typically alone. What I remember most was that I felt safe and full of wonder about the serene beauty around me.

One particular trek into the orchard comes to mind. It was winter, and the snow was falling lightly. I remember walking into the orchard and settling down in the middle of the place. I sat quietly, practicing what in Japanese is called *shinrin-yoku*, or what in English is called forest bathing. Though I didn't have the concept in mind at that time, "forest bathing" is essentially what I was doing. The place was silent, and no wind or noises disrupted this serene moment. I could literally hear the snow softly falling around me. I was filled with awe and sheer joy.

Discovering Spirituality

I've spent much of my life wandering through forests and settling quietly to let the surroundings bathe me with serenity. Those treks, like my wanderings into the apple orchard in early childhood, were soothing and awe-inspiring. They were transcendental moments that dissolved my sense of self and left me feeling at one with my surroundings. I now consider these moments as spiritual experiences that cultivated a deep sense of wonder and a commitment to pursue compassion and joy in my life.

Let me be clear. I make a sharp distinction between spirituality and religiosity. Although not new, that distinction grew out of my long experience with mainstream Judeo-Christian traditions. My great-grandfather, a Lutheran minister, emigrated to the United States from Denmark and built a Lutheran church in the suburbs of Kansas City. He later moved to California and started another Lutheran church. My mother grew up as a Lutheran, only to change religious affiliation when she married my father. They both joined an American Baptist church, which became the religious organization for the upbringing of my three sisters and myself.

Having four children and a struggling family business, my father supplemented his income by singing in a paid quartet in three different churches: his own Baptist church, a Methodist church, and an Episcopalian church. Sunday mornings became a traveling show from church to church, and I was a willing traveler, becoming exposed to different takes on the same Jesus. Besides these religious organizations, my paternal grandfather was active in the Unity Universal church, my paternal grandmother was a Catholic prior to marrying my grandfather, and my great-great-grandmother was Jewish. So, suffice to say I descended from a garden variety of religious traditions.

In short, my involvement with these religious organizations laid the foundation for a spiritual awakening, although it didn't get me all the way there. Obstacles to my spiritual growth included too much preoccupation with the organization itself, like running a business, and too many "dos" and "don'ts" embedded in various theologies and religious practices I'm not criticizing organized religions. They obviously work for countless people and have for centuries. They just didn't work for me. The forest served as a more effective spiritual sanctuary.

My Academic Journey (In Brief)

Growing up, I never considered myself a serious student. My K-to-12 years were marked by average grades and a noncommittal attitude about learning. I did just enough to get by. I loved any activity in the great outdoors, including organized sports such as track & field or football, but participation in sports ended with an injury. The focus during my teens then turned to working for extra money to buy a car, clothes, and whatever was needed to have fun with my friends. After graduating from high school, I did what was expected by my parents and peers alike. I went off to college. But my first two years there were much like the past, as I did just enough to get by while having fun.

Things changed after those first two years. Mind you, these were turbulent times, with the Vietnam War, various protests, and the civil rights movement. The events of that time began to raise my consciousness. Thinking critically about what was occurring became a preoccupation and provided the motivation to delve more deeply into my studies. As a journalism major, writing had become habit. But then I added a second major: sociology.

Adding my second major was a liberating move. Readings in that field opened the door to new perspectives on living. Before, I'd viewed humans as being like actors on a stage, only we don't know we're members of the play. But the sociological perspective allowed me to realize that we are more than this. We can break away from the social script and choreograph our own actions. That thought was liberating; it led me to pursue my PhD in sociology and eventually land my career as a professor.

From the Dark Side Springs the Light

Although I've taught basic courses in the social sciences throughout my career, studying violence was my primary teaching and scholarly focus. That's what I mean by the "dark side." Most of my violence research took place in research centers. I studied many types of violence, including political violence, especially in a cross-cultural context; criminal violence, particularly homicide; youth violence, with a focus on bullying; and domestic violence, specifically intimate partner violence.

What did I learn from this scholarly journey? Broadly defined, I discovered that, despite the diversity, all forms of violence seemed to be driven primarily by naked self-interest, vested-interest, or group-interest. This destructive behavior seemed to be either retaliation to grievances or the brutal pursuit of power to dominate and control others, including their lives, possessions, and places. I also learned that the many faces of violence persist, suggesting that despite efforts to understand, prevent, or reduce this behavior, our accomplishments haven't been stunning.

I was left wandering on the dark side of life, teaching and researching violence. I longed for the light that might bring hope to humanity. I began to think that perhaps violence, or more broadly, human cruelty, could be lessened if we would just listen to others without judgment and without the distraction of our own voice. Perhaps human cruelty would subside if we could simply understand others from their point of view, how they think, what they feel, the ways in which they suffer, and develop a willingness to accept, appreciate, and allow others to be as they are, addressing their suffering as needed.

I also began to think that the same things can be done with our own selves. We can address our suffering and more willingly accept, appreciate, and allow ourselves to be *who we are* as individuals. After all, compassion begins with ourselves.

Moving from the darkness to the light is a brief way of describing my motivation for co-authoring this book. I moved from *thinking* about what and how human cruelty can be prevented to *doing* something about it. I'm now more focused on what is good in us instead of what is evil, on building harmony and joy rather than the hatred and divisiveness so common in our world today.

Nancy's Story

In contrast to Kirk's childhood, mine was filled with more unpleasant memories than pleasant ones. I did have family around me, but some were driven by anger, while others were driven by fear of that anger. I'm honestly not sure how I emerged with such a loving heart. Even as a small child I couldn't understand why people hurt those they loved.

My father was a particularly stern disciplinarian who whipped me with his belt for even the smallest infractions. And I was by no means a bad child; I was full of energy, happiness, and love. Like all children, I sometimes talked too loud or jumped too high, but I never did anything truly bad so to speak. So at a very young age, perhaps five or six, I started to wonder why people were so mean to each other. And right there I vowed to myself to do the best I could to be helpful and kind. Somehow, compassion came to me on its own.

I was fortunate to have a set of personal attributes that enabled me to succeed during my childhood and adolescence. I always loved learning, was considered smart, made friends easily, and did well in sports. Unlike my home life, school was a very positive experience for me. My successes easily outnumbered my failures, and I grew to be a confident, self-directed, and self-assured young woman. Perhaps because others in my family were so harsh to themselves and to each other, self-compassion also came to me on its own. I saw failure as an opportunity to learn and do better rather than a time for self-criticism. I strived to be better than I was, not to be better than others. I measured my accomplishments against myself, not against others or some objective standard of excellence.

My family did not follow an organized religion, and I had no religious or spiritual training of any kind. But similar to Kirk, nature became my grounding and guidance. Although I grew up in the heart of urban Los Angeles, pretty much in a concrete jungle, I remember a small patch of grass with a lone tree in the front of my apartment. I used to sit on the grass and look at the tree and the sky, imagining I was walking in a forest full of trees. When I was old enough to ride the bus, I would go to the beach every day in summer and listen to and watch the ocean, imagining I was floating in time and space with the crashing of each wave. I remember also going to the Griffith Observatory and being fascinated by the stars and planets, memorizing and looking each night for the major constellations and being mesmerized by the vastness of the universe.

The College Years

In college, my interest in how people understood the world around them, interacted with each other, and found meaning and purpose in life led me to the field of psychology. But it also was the 1970s, when issues of justice and equality took center stage. From protesting the Vietnam War to marching for women's rights, my interest in individual behavior expanded to an interest in how we create a more fair and just society. This drew me to read and learn about moral philosophy, moral psychology, and the moral underpinnings of religious teachings, all of which led me to my graduate studies with Lawrence Kohlberg, one of the leading moral psychologists of the time. I had a very simple question I wanted answered: How can we get people to treat each other with honor, respect, and kindness?

During this time, I also became increasingly sensitized to the manner in which animals were raised and killed for us to eat them. I started not eating meat and quickly moved into what would now be called strict veganism. I felt it was morally unjustifiable to kill animals, often inhumanely, for our own benefit. I lasted for 10 years or so as a vegan, but somehow slowly inched back into eating fish, then eating hamburgers (which didn't look like an animal), then just trying my best not to eat meat. Honestly, it was simply too difficult to observe a rigid diet when out with friends, living with others who were not vegan, and navigating daily life. However, to this day I still would like to return to veganism at some point, and I do make sure the meat I eat is humanely raised in a normal and cage-free environment.

From the Lightness to the Dark Side and Back to the Light

My love of learning led me to a career in academia as a university professor. My intent was to continue studying kindness, compassion, and moral behavior. However, I quickly found that there was scant support, primarily in the form of research grants, for studying positive behavior. In contrast, concerns about aggressive behaviors, including school bullying and youth violence, loomed large, and funding was much more readily available. As it turned out, the department I was in had senior colleagues who studied aggression, and we collaborated on a large funded research grant. The project focused on the prevention of childhood aggression, and my contribution was to develop a social-emotional skills program that promoted virtues such as self-awareness, self-regulation, empathy, and prosocial behavior.

Clearly, a primary mechanism for preventing harmful behaviors is to cultivate helpful and prosocial behaviors. However, I became known as an aggression researcher. Most of the work I did, including presentations in the US and internationally, focused on preventing childhood aggression and youth violence. I felt like I was spending more time on the "dark side," and I wanted to shift my sole focus from preventing a negative to promoting a positive.

It took many years for my work to shift to promoting compassion, again propelled by a fortuitous set of events. In my most recent professional position at UC Irvine, I was fortunate to connect with colleagues who were interested in compassion and how to promote it, including generous donors, primarily The Living Peace Foundation, who wished to fund these efforts (who also have generously provided funding to make this book open access). Together we developed a series of classes on the science and practice of compassion and started a comprehensive program, the Global Service Scholars, for undergraduates to learn about and practice compassion around the globe. This program sent approximately 50 University of California undergraduates a year to perform services in sites ranging from an agricultural high school in Paraguay to a women's clinic in South Africa. The students also completed a year of coursework on compassion.

Although the service program proved difficult to sustain, I still teach an annual course on The Science and Practice of Compassion. I also regularly seek out engaging opportunities to learn and teach about compassion and fill my life with compassion and joy.

* * * *

Now you have a brief glimpse into our personal and professional lives and what we bring to writing this book. Through decades of work on preventing aggression and violence, we've learned that focusing on our common humanity is critical if we are to overcome the divisions that too often result in human cruelty and suffering. We hope to share what we have learned with you so you can bring compassion to the front and center of your world. We also hope to share with you many of the beautiful photos we've taken of our life together over the years (we took most of the photos in this book. You will see how much we love horses and the mountains).

The book is organized into three sections. We also recommend that you keep a *Compassion Journal* as you read through this book. You can write your reactions, things you want to remember, how what you are reading plays out in your own life, or any other thoughts or feelings you have.

In Part I, *The Case for Compassion*, we discuss the "what" and "why" of compassion. In Chapter 1, we describe the meaning and manifestations of suffering. We explore the connections between suffering and compassion to provide you with a deeper understanding of compassion and its roots. We look at different types of suffering, how alleviating suffering has played out across religions and cultures, and how our reaction to suffering involves perceiving, feeling, thinking, and getting ready to act. As we explain, compassion is complicated because it can be facilitated or derailed by our attentiveness and reactions to suffering.

In Chapters 2 and 3, we turn to why compassion is important. (These chapters rely heavily on research and are somewhat technical.) In Chapter 2, we look at the adaptive value of compassion and how it contributes to our survival. We discuss the evolutionary advantages of compassion, at the same time recognizing that evolution also places constraints on compassion. For instance, it is more adaptive to empathize with and help those in our closest groups or tribes, whom we can rely on in times of need. In Chapter 3, we look at the benefits of compassion for you. It's easy to see how compassion can help others, but it's also good for you! Indeed, research shows how compassion can make you happier, healthier, more creative, and bring joy into your life. Being compassionate can even change how your brain works.

In Part II, *The How of Compassion*, we dive into building blocks for living a compassionate life. In Chapter 4, we focus on "getting ready" and making space for compassion. We emphasize three steps: (1) decluttering both your external physical space and your internal psychic space; (2) reframing how you react to and understand the world; and (3) setting your intention to orient your life to compassion and joy.

In Chapter 5, we present the seven virtues of highly compassionate people, those being *mindfulness*, *self-awareness*, *gratitude*, *perspective taking*, *empathy*, *kindness*, and *altruism*. People who care about alleviating suffering and promoting well-being score high on some or all of these virtues. We also link these virtues together in a "Ladder of Compassion" that connects your perceptions, emotions, thoughts, and motivation to act. You can improve at these virtues, and we offer suggestions on how to do so.

In Chapter 6, we focus on self-compassion, how we treat ourselves. As we point out, self-compassion is not the same as self-absorption or being egotistical; it is being caring and loving to yourself because you are part of our common humanity. Ironically, for many people, self-compassion is even harder than being compassionate towards others. In Chapter 7, we review different ways to extend compassion to others. These range from simple practices and techniques you can use on a daily basis to specific strategies for extending compassion across different aspects of our lives, from childrearing to the workplace to more global applications.

In Part III, *Moving Forward*, we consider challenges to acting in a compassionate manner and leading a compassionate life. In Chapter 8, we consider barriers to compassion like compassion collapse and compassion fatigue. Have you ever turned away from images or stories about mass suffering? That is compassion collapse. As the number of victims of suffering increases, we become *less* compassionate. Just think about calls to help for children who are suffering. Do they show mass images of suffering or a single child who you can specifically help? We also discuss compassion fatigue, meaning the sheer exhaustion of being compassionate on a daily basis, typically experienced by those in the helping professions such as social workers, nurses, and physicians. We add our thoughts about less discussed roadblocks to compassion, such as men living by the behavioral expectations of masculinity.

In Chapter 9, we bring this all back to where we started, reflecting on how to build on the seven virtues to create something like a "symphony of the soul." As we discuss, a symphony requires multiple steps or movements and is characterized by a harmonious combination of elements. A compassion-driven life has a very complex topography that spans our thoughts, feelings, and actions. It requires a delicate inner harmony and musical score that is played in synchrony with the world around us.

* * * *

Our journey to understand and practice compassion in our life shows us that, like a puzzle, compassion has many different pieces. In this book, we try to bring the pieces together to inspire you as we have been inspired. We do this by drawing on multiple sources, ranging from religion and philosophy to the social and behavioral sciences. We share with you quotes from people who have inspired us and encourage you to search for what inspires you. We hope you realize, as we have, that living a life of compassion is the pathway to peace, harmony, unity, and joy for all sentient beings, beginning with ourselves.

A beautiful sunset in Southern California. A great way to experience awe in nature.
Source: © Nancy Guerra and Kirk R. Williams

Notes

1 www.dalailama.com/messages/world-peace/the-global-community
2 Brown, B. (2021). *Atlas of the heart.* Random House, p. 117.
3 Tutu, D. & Abrams, D. (2016). *The book of joy: Lasting happiness in a changing world.*
   Penguin/Random House.

References

www.dalailama.com/messages/world-peace/the-global-community
Brown, B. (2021). *Atlas of the heart.* Random House, p. 117.
Tutu, D. & Abrams, D. (2016). *The book of joy: Lasting happiness in a changing world.*
   Penguin/Random House.

PART I
THE CASE FOR COMPASSION

1

THE COMPASSION CURE

As we discussed in the prologue, compassion is both desire and action to prevent or reduce suffering. Indeed, compassion is the best cure for suffering.

Living a life of compassion means continuously building your strengths, virtues, and talents, and combining those with your understanding of suffering in its various forms, to make a difference, however big or small. It also means you try your best to do good in the world, that is, to be kind and considerate to all living things, to promote peace and harmony, and to care for and respect the planet.

Let's reflect a little more on suffering. What comes to mind when you think about suffering? How do *you* define it? If you're like most people, you probably think of big-picture disasters and the catastrophic consequences of such large-scale devastation, for example, hurricanes, wildfires, or mass famine. You also may think about extremely painful events like a prolonged illness or the loss of a loved one. But suffering comes in many forms, varying in intensity and duration.

Sometimes suffering is easy to spot, while other times it is subtle and even invisible. It also extends from ourselves to those close to us, to those beyond our inner circle, and to the entire planet. Suffering can be temporary and amenable to action, such as when we make up with a loved one after an argument. But it can also be long-standing and difficult to

DOI: 10.4324/9781003312437-2

3

Figure 1.1 The Taj Mahal in India—immense beauty against a backdrop of incredible suffering, where more than 20,000 people worked for 22 years and many died.
Source: © Nancy Guerra and Kirk R. Williams

endure, such as coping with a long and difficult illness or trying to right the wrongs inflicted from centuries of racism and injustice.

Unintentional Versus Intentional Suffering

One distinction we find useful in guiding our actions is that between suffering beyond our control (unintentional suffering) and suffering caused directly by our actions (intentional suffering).

Unintentional Suffering

Suffering, a fundamental part of living, is often beyond our control. The inevitability of suffering is a theme that cuts across history, philosophy, and religion. Indeed, most major religions tackle both the inevitability of suffering and the need to reduce it, cope with it, and learn from it. Natural disasters lead to extreme devastation and hardship. The consequence of love is grief and loss. Accidents happen; people get sick. Everyone fails at something during their lifetime. Of course, we can try to reduce the likelihood of these events by taking good care of ourselves and our planet, but we will never completely eradicate suffering in all its many forms.

Suffering can also provide an opportunity for learning, growth, and understanding. A central theme of existentialism is that to live is to suffer, and to survive is to find meaning in the suffering. The Jewish psychiatrist Viktor Frankl, who wrote specifically about surviving life in a concentration camp in his book, *Man's Search for Meaning*, notes that suffering ceases to be suffering at the moment it finds meaning. As Nietzsche famously said, "Out of life's school of war—what doesn't kill me, makes me stronger."[1]

People sometimes experience catastrophic illnesses or accidents, yet ultimately find their lives become richer and more full of gratitude as a consequence of their suffering. We often hear stories from survivors who look not only at how their life has changed for the worse, but often appreciate how their experience of suffering has made their life better. One's physical quality of life may decrease, but this is often accompanied by a renewed sense of gratitude for just being alive, and a renewed sense of clarity and purpose. Ironically, on the other hand, we frequently hear stories of people who win large lotteries and find themselves richer financially but unhappier than they've ever been.

Compassion drives us to help ourselves and others cope with suffering that is beyond our control, but *how* we help depends specifically on both the origins of suffering and our capacity to help. For instance, if your friend has lost a loved one and you have developed your empathy skills, simply setting aside time to be with your friend, to listen and understand what they are going through, is likely the best display of compassion. If your friend has lost her house in a fire, and you have an extra room, being kind and helpful by providing a place for her to stay clearly demonstrates compassion. Or if you just failed an important exam, being mindful (in the moment and without judgment), focusing on your strength and resilience, and thinking about failure as a learning experience can help you bounce back and try again.

Intentional Suffering

Sad as it sounds, humans cause a lot of suffering to themselves, others, and the planet. One need only look at our historical landscape, littered with its numerous forms of human cruelty and suffering. If we could jump in a time machine and travel backwards, we would see that early civilizations without stable forms of cities and governments routinely engaged in rampant and intentional cruelty, such as pilfering, raiding, feuding, dueling, and superstitious killing of people and animals. As societies became more developed, **violence and cruelty actually have declined over time**, as Stephen Pinker describes in his landmark book, *The Better Angels of Our Nature: Why Violence Has Declined*.

Still, the contemporary landscape and the not-too-distant past are filled with countless stories of humans causing suffering to others. The most glaring example can be seen in historical and contemporary events involving genocide, the deliberate mass killing of people from a particular national, religious, or ethnic group. For example, during WWII, the Nazis killed over six million Jews, exterminating about two-thirds of Europe's Jewish population. However, one of the most overlooked examples of genocide occurred in the late 1800s and early 1900s in what was then called the Congo Free State. An estimated 10 million Congolese people died because of forced labor and violent coercion used in the extraction of rubber cheaply and to maximize profits by King Leopold II of Belgium. In the 1990s, we witnessed the mass extermination of about 800,000 ethnic Tutsis in Rwanda by ethnic Hutu extremists. Recent years have seen rampant cruelty and destabilization in Afghanistan after the US military withdrew. We also have major displacement of populations because of the invasion of Ukraine by Russia, the military battle in Sudan, and the ongoing conflict in Tigray in Ethiopia.

In addition to the massive suffering we leave in our wake, humans cause suffering on a smaller scale to ourselves and others around us, including those we love. Thousands of people per year in the United States take their own lives, as do people in other countries across the globe.

We also take the lives of others. And surprisingly, we often hurt or kill those close to us and those we presumably love. For example, the CDC estimated that slightly over one-third of women have been assaulted or

Figure 1.2 Robben Island, South Africa. Where Nelson Mandela suffered in a cell for 27 years. Source: © Nancy Guerra and Kirk R. Williams

stalked by their intimate partners in their lifetime; when women are murdered, their intimate partners were the killers in approximately 40% of their deaths.

We all too frequently collectively legitimize the suffering of large groups of people through cultural norms, practices, policies, and laws. A striking example is the dark history of chattel slavery in the United States. This notorious institution denied human dignity to people identified as Black by legally dehumanizing them as chattel, meaning personal property that could be bought and sold. The 1787 Constitutional Convention rendered those enslaved as three-fifths of a person for purposes of taxation and representation in Congress. Legal chattel slavery persisted for over two centuries until the 13th Amendment was passed in 1865.

Then there is what might be called "suffering by neglect." What does that mean? In some cases, we cause suffering by either looking the other way or pushing responsibility onto others. For instance, in the early 2020s it is estimated that there are hundreds of thousands of homeless people in the United States. Although many efforts are underway to help them, other efforts push them away. Many cities fail to respond in a kind and helpful manner. In 2022, the National Law Center on Homelessness and Poverty found that about half of the cities they were monitoring had enacted laws that make it hard or nearly impossible to live in vehicles, even though these may be someone's only shelter.

Compassion drives us *to prevent* intentional suffering by any means necessary. Sometimes this means understanding the unique cultural and historical experiences of different groups and just being mindful of things you say or words you use, such as avoiding microaggressions. And in other cases, we feel compelled to make a bigger difference, to join a social movement or run for office to undo injustice and promote justice.

The important point is that intentional suffering is not a fundamental consequence of being human. It's a place where we can all make at least a small difference every day by extending kindness instead of cruelty to ourselves and others.

The Compassion Cure

If we want to alleviate as much suffering as we can, compassion is a good place to start. However, compassion is complicated and has many moving parts. First, you must *pay attention to suffering* to recognize it and remember it for longer than a few seconds. You also must feel an *emotional response* that triggers a desire to act. Compassion requires making *decisions* about whether those involved deserve or even desire your concern and whether you have the ability to do something. Taken together, your perceptions, emotions, and decisions can inspire you to *take action*.

Pay Attention to Suffering

Consider the attentional part of compassion. What impacts the likelihood that we will attend to the suffering of others? To begin, we must know that someone is suffering. This recognition is more likely when suffering is easily seen and when those suffering are people we see regularly. Your cousin is gravely ill. Your friend was in a car accident. Seeing suffering becomes more difficult when suffering is not readily apparent, either because we don't cross paths with those who suffer or because their suffering is hard to spot.

What if your neighbor is constantly berated and demeaned by her partner? You might not see any signs of her suffering and would only know about it if she told you. We've also learned the old adage "sticks and stones can break my bones but words can never hurt me" simply isn't true. Words can hurt, and we often fail to recognize the harm they cause. Why do we call incarcerated people "inmates" and give them numbers rather than names? Why have we called undocumented immigrants "illegal aliens?" What other forms of suffering can you think of that are pervasive but not readily apparent or visible?

Paying attention to suffering is more difficult beyond our immediate social circle. We often learn about the suffering of people we don't intimately know through different media channels. Yet, media coverage of suffering is uneven. Mass shooting in public places spark national multiday news coverage, public outcries for more restrictive gun control measures, flags flying at half-mast, sorrowful stories about the deceased victims, and heartfelt recollections of their survivors. Yet when 20 young men are killed in smaller, isolated incidents across Chicago, Detroit, and Baltimore over the course of a month, their deaths barely make the news.

Figure 1.3 On a Fulbright-sponsored visit to Tromso, Norway, where the climate crisis has drastically shortened the winter season. Global estimates predict that within nine or so years the effects of climate change will be irreversible.
Source: © Nancy Guerra and Kirk R. Williams

Mass shootings are of course devastating tragedies, yet they represent only a small fraction of yearly injuries or deaths by firearms (typically representing no more than *2% of gun-related injuries and less 0.1% of gun-related deaths*). Let that sink in. We dwell on the suffering of mass shooting victims and their families, but why does the suffering of thousands of homicide and suicide victims remain in the dark?

Beyond our differential exposure to suffering via the media, we humans are good at normalizing all kinds of suffering. This leads us to minimize the attention we give to suffering. Ask yourself this: How is it that in a country as wealthy as the United States (or other higher-income countries), large numbers of people go to bed hungry or wind up homeless? The truth is that we are more likely to turn our attention away from suffering as the number of victims increases (see Chapter 8 for a discussion of compassion collapse) or as it becomes so expansive that we can no longer wrap our heads and hearts around it, such as with the multiple consequences of global warming.

Different Emotions Lead to Different Reactions

We turn our attention away from suffering in part because suffering triggers a range of emotional reactions, both negative and positive (or energizing). A common negative reaction is distress, which causes us to shift our focus away from suffering and divert our attention to something else. Have you ever looked the other way when passing homeless people on the street, trying to avert their gaze? Or have you changed the channel when those ASPCA commercials of starving and shivering animals come on? Your emotional reaction to suffering can put the brakes on your attentional response. So, what's the key to combatting such a muted expression? You must attend to but not be emotionally overwhelmed by the suffering you witness.

Alternatively, our emotional reactions may trigger compassion. For example, seeing injustice may trigger outrage that makes us want to reduce that injustice. Seeing others in pain may lead to sadness that makes us want to help. One of the most widely discussed emotional reactions to suffering that motivates compassion is our capacity to feel *empathy*. Indeed, we are biologically wired to be emotionally entangled with others, to feel what they feel even before we are aware of it. That's what empathy is: feeling what others feel, whether sadness and sorrow or happiness and joy.

Think about the last time you heard a child cry. How did you react? Or how did you react the last time a friend glowed with exuberant joy? Feeling another's suffering moves us to react, to take the next step, to do something as if it were happening to us.

Paying attention to the suffering of others doesn't always trigger an empathic response, though. Why not? Just as our attention to suffering is influenced by different factors, so is the likelihood that we will react empathically. To start with, it's hard to empathize with more than a few people at the same time. If you see images of hundreds of starving children, would you react differently than if you see a picture of one little girl's hollowed face? There is a strategic reason that charities show pictures and tell stories about individuals rather than large groups. It's because you can understand the plight of hundreds mentally, but you can't truly empathize with them on such a large scale.

Just as you are more likely to feel empathy for a few people rather than many, single and novel events can spark the desire to help more than the constant drone of suffering. Why does a puppy in a well generate more news coverage than the thousands of abandoned dogs who land in shelters each year? Why are we glued to the television watching the rescue of eight miners trapped underground, yet we worry little about how many people die in mines each year (over 15,000 worldwide)? If we are subject to a regular barrage of suffering, we often become numb to it. It becomes almost like background noise, in part to reduce the emotional distress of dealing with it all of the time.

We also are more likely to respond with empathy when those who suffer are close to or similar to us, whether that means family and friends, neighbors, or others who belong to our social groups. As we note in various chapters in this book, empathy favors the "in-group" over the "out-group," a finding supported by studies of human evolution and confirmed by neuroscience research. Yet, if we are moved to act only when we feel some sense of kinship or connection with others in our own group, how can experiencing empathy foster compassion for all living beings? How can we extend empathy to all forms of life?

Thoughts Matter

Our responses to suffering, however, go beyond our attention and our feelings. What we think, our values and beliefs, also determines how we react and what we do. Certain traditions even believe that suffering, in essence, is largely a product of the mind. For example, in Buddhist teachings, our thoughts are at the very core of suffering: what you think is what you become. Suffering includes not only physical and mental pain from inevitable stressors, but also the suffering that comes from our thoughts and beliefs.

From a Buddhist perspective, we go through life grasping at what we *think* will satisfy our desires, but everything is transient, and we can never really hold on. We create our own suffering with an undisciplined and untamed mind that allows negative thoughts and emotions, such as anger and hatred, to flood our lives. We become toxic, which impacts us and those around us. But suffering can be minimized by cultivating a disciplined mind through, for example, mindfulness, mental alertness, and meditation. We can quell the suffering we cause ourselves and free ourselves of toxicity. Even physical pain becomes less stressful with the awareness of a disciplined mind.

A somewhat different perspective emphasizes how we can use our thoughts and beliefs to justify reactions ranging from inflicting suffering to looking the other way to responding with compassion. Think about examples where we justify suffering, such as capital punishment. On the surface, it seems almost absurd to punish someone who took a life by doing exactly the same thing to them. This is a central argument put forth by those who oppose capital punishment: that killing is wrong in and of itself. Others support capital punishment because they believe it is important to deter future crimes against the innocent. In their eyes, although we are causing suffering, we are preventing future suffering (even though the scientific evidence doesn't support this). Most frequently, support comes from the belief that the punishment fits the crime, that if you commit an egregious murder you deserve nothing less than death yourself. This is the essence of retributive justice, as reflected in the adage "An eye for an eye."

Revenge and retaliation as well as morally justifying suffering has a long history. These have been central themes in religious teachings, literature (Shakespeare was obsessed with revenge), moral philosophy, and politics. War is a good example. There are times when war is considered justifiable by a substantial number of people, and there are times when it is not. War in self-defense is seen as morally justified because a government owes the people the duty of protection.

But war is not justified if it is out of hatred or greed. And even when force is seen as justified, there are legal and international rules of engagement detailing how and when it can be used, just as the Eighth Amendment guarantees that the manner of death in capital punishment may not inflict unnecessary suffering or pain on the person being executed. As Aaron said in Shakespeare's *Titus Andronicus:* "Vengeance is in my heart, death in my hand, Blood and revenge are hammering in my head."[2]

We also decide whether the person or persons suffering are worthy of our response. Sometimes this is a categorical distinction many of us make automatically. For instance, children and the elderly are often seen as more worthy of compassion than adults, as they are less able to fend for themselves. In general, we tend to care more about people like us, leading us to evaluate what we have in common with those who are suffering. Do they look like us, live in our neighborhood, or share our political or religious affiliations?

Sometimes our reactions to suffering are based on whether we believe people are responsible for their own suffering, either through their actions or inactions. Studies have shown that when we believe people have brought on their own problems or aren't working very hard to solve them, we are less likely to help. For example, in a study conducted over 25 years ago, P.A. Dooley found that students who read a story about a person diagnosed with AIDS who had contracted the disease through a blood transfusion felt more compassion than participants who believed it was caused by unprotected sex or drug use.[3]

Taking Action

Just as we think about whether the person suffering deserves our compassion, we also think about and evaluate the urgency of the situation and our capacity and willingness to respond. A person drowning in a lake calls for immediate action, but if we can't swim, we won't jump in. Most of us will try to do at least something, although circumstances matter. For instance, many studies of the *bystander effect* find that people are less willing to intervene if there are other people present. We are less likely to take on the responsibility to help if we can pass it off to others, and as the number of bystanders increases, the likelihood of our intervening decreases.

What we feel and what we think determines, in part, our motivation to act. That action could be doing something to cause suffering, looking away, or taking action to alleviate suffering. Much has been written about the importance of our feelings, particularly of whether we feel empathy or empathic concern. A number of research studies find consistent support for the *empathy-altruism hypothesis*, which states that empathic concern leads to altruistic (rather than egoistic) motivation and action. Not only has empathic concern been found to motivate helping behavior, but it also improves the quality of the help.

Empathy alone will not save the world, even though in recent years many suggest it is the antidote to almost all social ills. You don't need to feel the pain of someone pinned under a car to rush to their aid. In some cases, we are convinced by science and reason alone. Just watch a documentary about climate change, food insecurity, or meat processing, and you likely will feel at least a temporary sense of motivation to do something to help. Alternatively, you may actually feel what someone is feeling but not have the desire, capacity, or willingness to do anything to help.

Not everyone is affected the same way in the face of suffering. Some people are swayed more by their emotions, while others are motivated more by reason. Some situations evoke a specific emotional response, while others connect to a more general belief about the importance of promoting the well-being of others and our planet. As we said, compassion is complicated. So is translating our feelings and thoughts into the best course of action, one that combines our hearts and our heads. As we shall discuss in more detail later in Chapters 5 and 7, this is the notion behind "effective altruism."

The basic principle of effective altruism is that the heart can motivate you to do good, but the head must motivate you to follow the course of action that will have the greatest impact and that aligns with your skills and values. For example, if you are really good at financial planning, the most effective course of action might be to make as much money as you can as a financial planner and donate a significant amount of your earnings to high-impact charities.

* * * *

Our apologies if we've tested your patience by taking you through the nuances of suffering and compassion. But as you'll see in later chapters, the distinctions we've mapped out are important in understanding how we respond. Do we constructively engage suffering to mitigate it? Do we ignore it? Or do we think someone deserves it? Are we overwhelmed by it, exhausted by it, or have we neglected it? Do we ever cause it?

You may think that practicing compassion is easier said than done. Perhaps you have experienced times of great adversity and been overwhelmed by what it takes to survive. But, under such circumstances, feeling unhappy, sad, or angry for long periods of time will never help you overcome the situation. On the contrary, it may lead only to anxiety, despair, and self-protection. It may even eat away at you or push you to act harshly or aggressively towards yourself or others, thus creating even more suffering.

Despite the complexity of suffering we've talked about, let us close this chapter with some comforting thoughts. No matter how suffering varies across time and place, and no matter how others respond to suffering, you have the power to recognize it in yourself, in others, and in your surroundings. A common theme in this book is that compassion begins where you are, at home, in yourself. As we will see in Chapter 6, only by recognizing and responding to the suffering in your life can you begin to recognize and respond to the suffering of those you love, those around you, and even those far away. Creating a life driven by compassion is not an end-goal; it is a lifelong journey that starts with you.

Consider the insightful words of Thich Nhat Hanh:

> If we take care of the suffering inside us, we have more clarity, energy, and strength to help address the suffering violence, poverty, and inequity of our loved ones as well as the suffering in our community and the world … There is an art to suffering well. If we know how to take care of our suffering, we not only suffer much, much less, we also create more happiness around us and in the world.
>
> (p. 13)[4]

Figure 1.4 The peaceful beauty of the night sky in the mountains.
Source: © Nancy Guerra and Kirk R. Williams

Notes

1 F. Nietzsche, (1889/1997). *Twilight of the idols.* Hackett.
2 Shakespeare, William. 1564–1616. (2000). *Titus Andronicus.* Penguin Books.
3 Dooley, P. A. (1995). Perceptions of the onset controllability of AIDS and helping judgments: An attributional analysis. *Journal of Applied Social Psychology, 25* (10), 858–869.
4 Thich Nhat Hanh (2019). *No mud, no lotus: The art of transforming suffering.* Parallax Press, p. 13.

References

Dooley, P. A. (1995). Perceptions of the onset controllability of AIDS and helping judgments: An attributional analysis. *Journal of Applied Social Psychology, 25*(10), 858–869.

Nietzsche, F. (1889/1997). *Twilight of the idols.* Hackett.

Shakespeare, William. 1564–1616. (2000). *Titus Andronicus.* Penguin Books.

Thich, Nhat Hanh (2019). *No mud, no lotus: The art of transforming suffering.* Parallax Press, p. 13.

2
BORN TO CARE

As we discussed in Chapter 1, both the historical record and contemporary events speak to our capacity to cause harm to others and to legitimize or ignore even the most extreme types of suffering. Fortunately, we also have an enormous capacity to care for others—to demonstrate empathy, kindness, and generosity and to alleviate suffering. Compassion and related virtues such as empathy and kindness are inherent to our very being. Not only do they make our lives better, but they also contribute to our survival as a species. Imagine a world where no one understood or cared about your feelings, where kindness didn't exist and no one lent a helping hand to those who suffer. We doubt you (or anyone) would want to live in this world. It's unlikely anyone could even *survive* in such a world.

That's right: Evolution favors characteristics we inherit and that increase our chances of surviving and reproducing over generations. Living organisms that are best adapted to their environment are the likeliest to survive and pass on their genes. Although the notion of "survival of the fittest" may suggest the strongest, most competitive, or most aggressive individuals, it more correctly refers to those who are most capable of adapting to their environments. It is those individuals who have the greatest chance to pass their successful traits to offspring.

Evolution is complicated and sometimes a bit challenging to understand. We admit this chapter is fairly dense. However, the information

DOI: 10.4324/9781003312437-3

17

Figure 2.1 Firstborn. Tenderness from the first moments of life.
Source: © Nancy Guerra and Kirk R. Williams

provided will pay off in full in the long run, and you will find yourself a more compassionate, whole person after absorbing it.

What qualities make us most adaptable to our environments? There's much debate about the traits and behaviors linked to fitness and adaptability. Are the fittest those who are the most cunning and competitive, who want to win at all costs? Or is it the more sympathetic and cooperative members of society, those who work for the common good, who succeed? Answering this question has been one of the great challenges of evolutionary biology. If we view survival as a natural competition with winners and losers, a *Social Darwinist* approach, we might also wonder why cooperation should exist at all in such a world. This interpretation can lead us to justify all sorts of harmful behaviors such as racism, sexism, and oppression.

The most likely scenario is one where both aggressive and prosocial tendencies co-exist because of the evolutionary advantages they convey. If humans only inflicted pain and suffering on each other, without the ability to cooperate, connect, and alleviate suffering, we would most certainly destroy each other and the planet in short order. We could not survive in such a violent, harsh, and uncaring world. But just as we are biologically prepared for "fight or flight," we also are biologically prepared for kindness and collaboration, the seeds of compassion. As well-known ethologist Frans de Waal notes:

> In biology, the very same principle of natural selection that mercilessly plays off life forms and individuals against one

another, has led to symbiosis and mutualism among different organisms, to sensitivity of one individual to the needs of another, and to joint action toward a common goal. We are facing the profound paradox that genetic self-advancement at the expense of others—which is the basic thrust of evolution—has given rise to remarkable capacities for caring and sympathy.

(p. 5)[1]

The Adaptive Functions of Caring and Compassion

Most contemporary evolutionary accounts describe three primary adaptive functions of our prosocial tendencies to care for others and minimize suffering: (1) to enhance the welfare of vulnerable offspring; (2) to facilitate mate selection; and (3) to encourage collaborative and cooperative relations among individuals who are not related to each other, thereby enhancing our ability to live in large groups. Let's take a brief look at each one.

Enhancing the Welfare of Vulnerable Offspring

One of the most critical selection pressures shaping evolution is the need to care for the vulnerable, beginning with one's offspring. Getting our genes to the next generation requires safely raising our offspring to reproductive age. Because we are born more prematurely and are dependent on others longer than any other mammal, our chances of survival during infancy and childhood improve when we have a strong bond with a primary caregiver and strong ties to families and communities.

Both infants and caregivers have developed a range of biologically driven adaptive responses that promote caring and connection, allowing caregivers to respond quickly to signs of suffering. Just looking at babies makes most anyone smile. They are born cute, with big heads and eyes, chubby cheeks, a small chin, and soft skin. Scientists say these traits help infants survive by activating instinctual caregiving mechanisms in parents and adults.

Early displays of compassion also rely heavily on an elaborate system of communication. Think of the ways infants and their caregivers communicate with each other. They coo, babble, and speak gently to each

Figure 2.2 The same firstborn at four months, with a bright smile and eagerness to learn about the world.

Source: © Nancy Guerra and Kirk R. Williams

other; they use a range of facial expressions to signal distress and other emotions; and they are often in close physical contact with each other. We see these capacities at birth or very soon after.

For example, *mirror neurons* in an infant's brain allow them to mimic the facial expressions they see by the time they are three days old. We see these behaviors across totally different cultures, including in remote, pre-industrial societies. We even see them in bonobos and chimpanzees, which demonstrates the important role of caregiving in our closest, non-human primate relatives.

Soothing touch is a particularly adaptive mechanism in humans and nonhumans. In fact, touch has been shown to reduce levels of pain and stress and activate reward regions in the brain. When an infant begins crying, a common response is to gently touch them. We pick them up, embrace them, rock them, or stroke their hair or head. Non-human primates also use touch to communicate, spending almost a quarter of their day grooming each other and sharing food. Indeed, touch may be one of the first strategies we use to form cooperative bonds and reduce suffering in others. Just think about a time you've used a gentle touch to comfort someone who is suffering. You can likely recall a moment like that from your very recent past, right?

Scientists have asked whether a gentle touch can truly make us kinder and more generous. Have you ever heard of the Midas Touch Effect? Remember, Midas was a Greek mythological figure whose touch turned everything to gold. No, touch doesn't turn us into gold—but according

Figure 2.3 Soulmates Cliff and Mr. Darcy at Summit Valley Horse Center.
Source: © Nancy Guerra and Kirk R. Williams

to several scientific studies, casual touch promotes positive emotions and goodwill towards others.

For example, a classic social psychological study showed that customers at restaurants give bigger tips when they are lightly touched by their server.[2] In another study looking at the effect of touch, participants who were touched were more compliant when being asked to watch for a large and very excited dog while its owner was shopping.[3] Touch even prompted a bus driver to allow free rides to passengers.[4] Just think about how many social rituals that foster trust and collaboration involve touch, from handshakes to hugs to a pat on the back. Indeed, one of the challenges we currently face is how to allow gentle, compassionate touch that promotes well-being without crossing the line into unwanted or intrusive touching.

Evolution prepared us for caregiving in one other crucial way. It gave individuals with specific characteristics advantages in mate selection, thereby increasing the likelihood of passing on their genes to the next generation.

Mate Selection

If you were to list the most desirable characteristics in a mate, what would be at the top of the list? Here's what 10,000 participants across 37 nations said when David Buss, a well-known psychologist, asked them how important different attributes were in potential romantic partners.[5] At the top of their list was *kindness*.

If we look at our evolutionary history, kindness makes perfect sense. Humans began to collaborate actively with partners to obtain food some 400,000 years ago. Foraging for food required active engagement with a partner to form a joint goal—in other words, "putting one's head together" with another. Those who could not form connections with others and work collaboratively or those who hogged all the food were not chosen as partners. As a consequence, they were more likely to go hungry and eventually die. This led to a strong social selection for partners who were kind, cooperative, and collaborative.

Fast forward to modern society. Beyond helping with the grocery bills, kind people are more likely to devote resources to their offspring, spend time with them, provide physical care, and create positive, collaborative environments necessary for survival. We might also expect kind and compassionate partners to be faithful and commit to long-term monogamous bonds. Indeed, this preference for kindness has been replicated across a large number of research studies.

Still, there are some interesting caveats. In one study by Aaron Lukaszewski and James Roney, participants preferred partners who are kind and trustworthy when thinking about behaviors directed towards themselves or close friends and family. However, these same participants were less concerned about kindness and related behaviors when considering actions towards *non*-family members.[6] This leads us to consider how the evolutionary advantages of kindness and compassion towards those closest to us are (or are not) afforded to those who are not part of our immediate social circle.

If you had lived before the era of modern humans, some 150,000 years ago, most of your collaborative foraging and group activities would have been with your family and smaller groups of relatives or close friends. Sharing and equity were ubiquitous. In this manner, people could survive potential looming challenges, a kind of insurance policy against food shortages, illness, or the whims of nature. There were clear survival benefits of kindness and compassion towards those in your immediate social circle.

But as human populations grew, we began to organize into larger and more well-defined groups or tribes, which in turn led to a need for collaboration beyond one's immediate kin group. Within these tribes,

Figure 2.4 Working together in synchrony.
Source: © Nancy Guerra and Kirk R. Williams

comprised of kin and non-kin, people needed to work together. They had to work with each person having a stake in the welfare of others—not just the welfare of their immediate family. Those who were able to coordinate and work together with *both kin and non-kin* were more likely to succeed, survive, and pass on their genes to the next generation.

Formation of Cooperative Relations with Non-Kin

A third evolutionary argument suggests that the compassionate predilections of others are an important criterion in the formation of cooperative relations with non-kin (those not related to us). As we mentioned previously, our hominid ancestors were dependent on these cooperative relations to forage and hunt for food in small groups of kin and non-kin, to defend against predators and competitors from other groups, and to reproduce and ensure that offspring matured to the age where they could carry on their genetic lineage.

People who were able to get along better with group members and be good team players were more likely to survive and reproduce. Being part of a larger group meant doing things for the good of the group, even at a cost to the individual. Primitive systems of distribution were developed within groups that favored kindness over greed. People who were more agreeable, compassionate, helpful, and trustworthy were more likely to be in the good graces of others. Not only might they expect immediate reciprocity of good will (the notion of *reciprocal altruism*), but they would be more likely to develop a reputation as a helpful and compassionate person, leading others to treat them better (the notion of *indirect reciprocity*).

However, as societies expanded to have multiple different (and often competing) groups, social interactions became more complex. Loosely structured social groups evolved into tighter-knit communities to protect their group from outsiders. In-group/out-group distinctions became critical for survival. Our bias to favor those closest to us extended beyond our immediate family, but only as long as we could identify others as members of our in-group. We developed a whole set of norms, rituals, and beliefs to signify membership in our group.

Collaborative engagement within a bounded group enhanced our chances of survival because people are more likely to look out for members of their own groups, come to their aid, distribute labor effectively, and pool risk. Not only has this in-group favoritism been observed across a vast range of real-life social situations (and in non-human species), but we can also artificially create group distinctions simply by assigning people to one arbitrary group or another.

Decades of research have demonstrated these in-group/out-group biases and how they arise. For instance, the Robbers Cave experiment is an enduring social psychological study conducted by Muzafer Sherif and colleagues as part of a series of studies in the 1940s and 1950s. In this experiment, researchers looked at whether normal, well-adjusted boys at a summer camp who were randomly assigned to one of two competing groups would develop hostilities towards the out-group, and whether these in-group/out-group hostilities could be overcome by re-orienting the groups to focus on a common purpose.

When the boys arrived at camp, they were assigned to groups, housed in separate cabins, given group names, and spent a week interacting only with members of their group. The following week, the groups were allowed to interact with each other. What do you think happened? Do you think they bonded into a larger group? Or do you think that hostilities developed between the groups?

If you guessed that hostilities emerged, you are correct! The first sign of conflict was name-calling. The experimenters then increased the level of competition between the two groups, leading to derogatory songs and even group members refusing to eat in the same room as the other group. Fortunately, the groups reconciled, but only after they engaged in tasks that identified a common purpose (in a sense creating a new group identity).[7]

Ironically, this preference for the in-group also presents one of the greatest challenges for compassion. How do we extend our kindness and concern, our desire to alleviate suffering, beyond those in our in-group? How do we come to realize that we are all human beings with similar needs, desires, and challenges? In psychologist Paul Bloom's book, *Against Empathy: The Case for Rational Compassion*, he details how empathy most frequently is directed only to those in our in-groups. In fact, he claims that empathy actually *promotes* biases such as parochialism and racism because it directs us to focus on the here and now, to those we care most about. This often occurs at the expense of the outgroup, even becoming a force for war and atrocity towards others.[8]

Think about *your* life. Are you kinder to those you share a common set of beliefs, culture, or purpose with? What keeps you from extending your circle of care to all humans? Evolution, indeed, favors affiliation with those we are more tightly connected with. Perhaps as the world becomes more globalized and we share the challenges facing our planet, we will embrace the connections that can bring us all together.

Let's now observe how the evolutionary advantages of caring, cooperation, and a desire to alleviate the suffering of others gave rise to specific biological changes in humans. In other words, how did we evolve to be innately equipped for kind and caring relationships with others? What does our compassion circuitry look like? As C. Sue Carter and colleagues note in *The Oxford Handbook of Compassion Science*:

> As mammals evolved, they became increasingly dependent on social cues and social support from others, usually of their own species. Social behaviors allowed mammals to more safely eat, digest, sleep, mate, and care for their dependent young. The processes that led to the evolution of mammalian social engagement and communication, and in some species, compassion, were associated with the evolution of the neurobiology of the central and autonomic nervous system.
>
> (p. 174)[9]

Nature and Nurture

Compassion, which has a biological foundation in our brains and bodies, and related virtues have been shaping forces in human evolution for tens of thousands of years. Although nature has equipped a range of social species (from ants to rodents to chimps to elephants) with a rudimentary ability to display at least some primitive forms of caring behaviors, our sophisticated and nuanced displays of compassion depend on the uniquely human cognitive abilities we are born with. These processes develop over an extended period during childhood, adolescence, and adulthood as a consequence of both our biological circuitry and the culture and context in which we grow up. Compassion is not nature versus nature; it's a complex and continuous feedback loop between nature and nurture.

Our biologically-driven capacity for coordinating with others and responding to distress and suffering can be observed from the time we are born. Newborn babies cry when they hear another infant crying. Very young children try to comfort other children who are crying by offering hugs, toys, and other forms of visible concern. We are born with a brain that is capable of compassion. Scientists constantly are learning more about how specific regions of the brain function both independently and in concert with other regions to drive a wide range of caring behaviors, thus representing a common neural network for compassion.

For example, recent studies analyzed regions of the brain associated with *empathy*. Researchers identified the *cerebral cortex*—specifically the *anterior insular cortex (AIC)*—as the area of the brain that is responsible for our ability to relate empathically to others. Scientists extended this work to identify abnormalities in these identifiable neural circuits associated with empathy deficits in brain injury patients. They also identified links to neuropsychiatric disorders characterized by social functioning difficulties, such as autism spectrum disorders, borderline personality disorder, and schizophrenia.[10]

The brain and the spinal cord are part of our central nervous system. We also have a peripheral nervous system, consisting mainly of nerves, that connects the central nervous system to all other parts of our body. It is within this system of nerves that we find another potential source of compassion: *the vagus nerve*. The vagus nerve is part of the parasympathetic branch of the autonomic nervous system (a subsystem of the peripheral nervous system). Think of this nerve as a superpower information highway that connects your mind and your body.

Why is the vagus nerve important for compassion? First of all, it helps you develop a healthy stress response and promotes resilience. A healthy vagal tone, a key contributor to the vagus nerve, is associated with greater emotion regulation, connection, calmness, and overall health and well-being. It also helps you remain calm and be less guarded in social interactions, serving as a brake on your heart rate. In addition, the vagus nerve is connected to oxytocin receptors, the building blocks of sociality, warmth, and trust. Psychologist Stephen Porges labeled the vagus nerve the "love nerve" because, when activated, it promotes love and kindness.

Studies have shown that exposure to distress and suffering—even just seeing brief images of harm—activates the vagus nerve. Fortunately, there are less disturbing ways to activate it than by staring at images of distress or listening to horrific stories. In fact, there is a growing body of evidence demonstrating that contemplative practices such as mindfulness meditation, humming, chanting, breathwork, and yoga improve vagal tone and make us more compassionate.

In a series of intriguing studies, psychologist Dacher Keltner identified what he called "vagal superstars." He predicted that individuals with high levels of vagus nerve activity would be active caretakers with extensive social connections who put compassion front and center in their lives. He and his colleagues tracked the lives of people identified as vagal superstars over several months. What they found was that the vagal superstars, compared with individuals with low baseline vagal tone, had more social connections, friendships, warmth towards others, optimism, and general positive mood. They also reported more transformative experiences associated with sacrifice, altruism, and connections with others.[11]

In addition to having a biological blueprint for compassion, we also develop our capacity to care about others through maturation and learning. Humans have a long period of extended immaturity lasting from infancy to early adulthood with large costs and risks for both caregivers and offspring. Fortunately, this lengthy period of maturation also has some adaptive advantages for fostering compassion. First and foremost, it gives us time to learn and refine a range of skills, attitudes, beliefs, and behaviors that help us adapt to the cultures and contexts in which we grow up. Consistent with modern evolutionary developmental biology, the target of natural selection is not just adult traits or behaviors but also the processes or ontogenetic pathways that bring them into existence.

Next, let's look at some examples of how our capacity for compassion unfolds from birth through the teenage years.

How Human Development Promotes Compassion

The long period of human development that spans from birth through adolescence allows for the unfolding of various adaptations. In combination, these adaptations strengthen our social bonds and increase our capacity for caring and compassion. They also reflect both the maturation of innate capacities and culture-bound social learning. Furthermore, it's important to keep in mind that there is considerable individual variation in biologically-driven capacities coupled with variation in cultural and environmental factors that impact their development. Let's consider some examples in infancy, childhood, and adolescence.

To begin with, babies (both animal and human) depend on secure attachments (i.e., a loving and trusting relationship with a primary caregiver). Have you heard of Harry Harlow's famous experiment with rhesus monkeys? They were given a choice between a soft terrycloth mother with no food and a wire mother who provided food. The monkeys were taken from their natural mother and raised by these new wire mothers. Who do you think they spent more time with? You're right if you said the cloth mother. They went to the wire mother for food but preferred to spend the rest of their time with the cloth mother. Follow-up studies showed that they also went to the cloth mother for comfort and security, highlighting the importance of the infant-caregiver bond beyond simply providing food, even in non-humans.[12]

In addition to the bond with a primary caregiver, infants quickly develop different abilities that foster interaction with others. At around six months of age, they can follow the gaze of close-in targets. This seems to be linked primarily to maturation, given that studies show consistency in gaze following across very different cultural contexts.[13] At around nine months of age, babies begin to engage in acts of joint intention—an important pathway for sharing psychological states with others—that continues to develop during the second year of life.

More elaborate social and cognitive skills develop alongside early language skills, around two to three years of age. By this time, children can imitate others' expressions, communicate relatively effectively, and coordinate their behavior with others—all important adaptations for living in a world with other children and adults. They also display sympathy for others, even beyond the immediate context of need, and allocate help selectively based on deservingness. These skills emerge without direct instruction and across different cultures, given presumably favorable social and environmental conditions.

Beginning around ages five to six, children are introduced more formally to the symbols, conventions, and gestures that serve standardized social interactions. They become more involved collaboratively with peers and begin to engage in joint problem solving, using rules, reasons, and justifications to coordinate their decision making with others. Notable in this age range is a fixation on the rules of the game as they learn the objective order of their world. Even if they are asked to play a game without rules, they quickly will make them up.

Children in this age group can take the perspective of the other in a two-person interaction; however, they are not yet capable of extracting themselves from the interaction and taking a third-person perspective. We can think of this period as the *age of reason*. Here, children are integrating the perspectives of peers and adults with their own needs and viewpoints to engage in collaborative problem solving and coordinated decision making with others.

Figure 2.5 During middle childhood and beyond children enjoy games with rules.
Source: © Freepik.com

During the middle childhood years and into adolescence, children come to understand that others are evaluating them, and they come to evaluate themselves, too. They display high levels of agreement with and conformity to the group, peaking during early adolescence as social cliques and in-group/out-group allegiances form. Much like the boys in the Robber's Cave experiment, cliques become tightly connected, often leading to hostility towards outsiders. At the same time, they recognize others as equals, and issues of fairness and equity loom large.

As humans move into the teenage years, they become more self-aware, better able to self-regulate their behavior, and increasingly able to take the third-person perspective—to look at a situation from the outside rather than the inside.

* * * *

As these examples suggest, the seeds of compassion are both innate and learned, with the early years being particularly important for learning to care for and collaborate with others. How do we capitalize on the abilities we are born with to create a more compassionate society? Although unrealistic, one suggestion would be to stick to a purely evolutionary perspective, with which we could selectively breed the most cooperative individuals with each other to bring about genetic change.

A more feasible approach, though, is to teach and reinforce compassion and related virtues and to create settings where these virtues are adaptive. What are the different contexts you navigate in daily? How could you modify these contexts so that compassion is an adaptive response? Whatever you choose to do or wherever you live, work, and play, there always is more you can do to make compassion work not only for you but for everyone you cross paths with.

Here are some other ideas.

To begin with, as we mentioned in the prologue, just being out in nature and experiencing the awe and wonder of our planet connects you with common humanity. From an evolutionary standpoint, natural spaces provided pre-modern humans with everything they needed to survive, such as food, comfort, and safety. In today's more urban and developed world, it still is likely that these spaces provide a similar sense of ease and help us get outside of ourselves. We know from many scientific experiments that being in nature, even just looking at pictures of nature, leads to relaxation and reductions in stress.

Now, think about a time when you were in charge of something, whether leading a group, teaching someone a skill, or taking care of children. How did you deal with their failures? Did you use those moments as an opportunity for learning and encouragement, or did you respond negatively? Berating someone for their failure only contributes to their suffering. Creating contexts where failure is an opportunity for learning and development spreads positivity and reduces suffering.

Another approach is to seek out places to work where compassion is practiced on a regular basis. Do you know what a B corporation (B Corp) is? It's a business certified by B Lab that meets a high standard of transparency, social, and environmental performance, and legal accountability to balance profit and purpose. It reflects the theme of *stakeholder capitalism*, where companies are responsible not only for profit but for the benefit of all stakeholders. B Lab was founded in 2006 by three friends who wanted to make business a force for good. In 2007 there were 82 certified B Corps; the number has grown to over 6,000 in early 2023. (We discuss these compassion-promoting settings in more detail in Chapter 7.)

Figure 2.6 A beautiful sunrise in Colorado. The warmth of the sky can comfort your soul.
Source: © Nancy Guerra and Kirk R. Williams

Notes

1   deWaal, F. (1997). *Good natured: The origins of right and wrong in humans and other animals.* Harvard University Press, p. 5.
2   Crusco, A. H. & Wetzel, C. G. (1984). The Midas Touch. The effects of interpersonal touch on restaurant tipping. *Personality & Social Psychology Bulletin, 10,* 512–517.
3   Guéguen, N. & Fischer-Lokou, J. (2003). Another evaluation of touch and helping behavior. *Psychological Reports, 92* (1), 62–64.
4   Guéguen, N. & Fischer-Lokou, J. (2003). Tactile contact and spontaneous help: An evaluation in a natural setting. *The Journal of Social Psychology, 143* (6), 785–787.
5   Buss, D. (1989). Sex differences in human mate preferences: Evolutionary hypothesis tested in 37 cultures. *Behavioral and Brain Sciences, 12,* 1–49.
6   Lukaszewski, A. & Roney, J. (2010). Kind toward whom? Mate preferences for personality traits are specific. *Evolution and Human Behavior, 31,* 29–38.
7   Sherif, M., Harvey, O. J., White, R. J., Hood, W., & Sherif, C. W. (2012). *The robbers cave experiment.* Wesleyan University Press.
8   Bloom, P. (2016). *Against empathy: The case for rational compassion.* Harper Collins.
9   Carter, C. Sue, Bartal, I., & Porges, E. C. (2017). The roots of compassion: An evolutionary and neurobiological perspective. In E. Seppala et al. (eds), *The Oxford handbook of compassion science.* Oxford University Press, p. 174.
10 Kennedy, D. & Adolphs, R. (2012). The social brain in psychiatric and neurological disorders. *Trends Cognitive Science, 16* (11), 559–572. doi: 10.1016/j.tics.2012.09.006
11 Keltner, D. (2012). *The compassionate species.* Berkeley, CA: Greater Good Science Center.
12 Harlow, H. F. & Zimmermann, R. R. (1958). The development of affective responsiveness in infant monkeys. *Proceedings of the American Philosophical Society, 102,* 501–509.
13 Callaghan et al. (2011). Early social cognition in three cultural contexts. *Monographs of the Society for Research in Child Development, 76* (2), 1–142.

References

Bloom, P. (2016). *Against empathy: The case for rational compassion.* Harper Collins.
Buss, D. (1989). Sex differences in human mate preferences: Evolutionary hypothesis tested in 37 cultures. *Behavioral and Brain Sciences, 12,* 1–49.
Callaghan et al. (2011). Early social cognition in three cultural contexts. *Monographs of the Society for Research in Child Development, 76*(2), 1–142.
Carter, C. Sue, Bartal, I., & Porges, E. C. (2017). The roots of compassion: An evolutionary and neurobiological perspective. In E. Seppala et al. (eds), *The Oxford handbook of compassion science.* Oxford University Press, p. 174.
Crusco, A. H. & Wetzel, C. G. (1984). The Midas Touch. The effects of interpersonal touch on restaurant tipping. *Personality & Social Psychology Bulletin, 10,* 512–517.
deWaal, F. (1997). *Good natured: The origins of right and wrong in humans and other animals.* Harvard University Press, p. 5.
Guéguen, N. & Fischer-Lokou, J. (2003). Another evaluation of touch and helping behavior. *Psychological Reports, 92*(1), 62–64.

Guéguen, N. & Fischer-Lokou, J. (2003). Tactile contact and spontaneous help: An evaluation in a natural setting. *The Journal of Social Psychology*, *143*(*6*), 785–7.

Harlow, H. F. & Zimmermann, R. R. (1958). The development of affective responsiveness in infant monkeys. *Proceedings of the American Philosophical Society*, *102*, 501–509.

Keltner, D. (2012). *The compassionate species*. Berkeley, CA: Greater Good Science Center.

Kennedy, D. & Adolphs, R. (2012). The social brain in psychiatric and neurological disorders. *Trends Cognitive Science*, *16*(*11*), 559–572. doi: 10.1016/j.tics.2012.09.006.

Lukaszewski, A. & Roney, J. (2010). Kind toward whom? Mate preferences for personality traits are specific. *Evolution and Human Behavior*, *31*, 29–38.

Sherif, M., Harvey, O. J., White, R. J., Hood, W., & Sherif, C. W. (2012). *The robbers cave experiment*. Wesleyan University Press.

3
Compassion Is Good for You

Would you like to be healthier, happier, more resilient, and live longer? Because a growing body of scientific evidence suggests that living your life with compassion front and center can have tremendous benefits for your physical and mental health, happiness, resilience, and longevity. Stated simply, compassion is good for you!

Think about a time when you did something to help another person and reduce their suffering. How did you feel? Were you sad and upset, or were you happy and content? It's quite likely the pleasure centers in your brain lit up, leading you to experience great pleasure. In fact, recent brain-imaging studies have shown that the parts of the brain that are active when we experience a broad range of pleasurable events (like eating chocolate or winning money) are equally active when we are helping others. It's called a "helper's high."

Much of the research on the health benefits of compassion focuses on specific components of compassion towards the self and others. As we mentioned earlier—and as we discuss in much more detail in Chapter 5—we have identified the "Seven Virtues" of highly compassionate people: self-awareness, mindfulness, gratitude, perspective taking, empathy, kindness, and altruism. The bulk of research on the benefits of compassion has focused on four of these virtues: mindfulness, gratitude, kindness, and altruism. Outcomes studied of having these virtues include a range

DOI: 10.4324/9781003312437-4

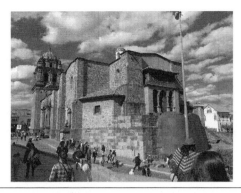

Figure 3.1 Cusco, Peru. On our way to Ayacucho, Peru with Global Service Scholars.
Source: © Nancy Guerra and Kirk R. Williams

of health benefits such as lower levels of stress, anxiety, and depression, lower blood pressure, a stronger immune system, enhanced recovery from illness, and increased longevity.

The Benefits of Mindfulness

Over the last decade or so, mindfulness almost has become a household term. Many of us are learning to pay attention in the moment, without judgment, to connect with and accept our thoughts and feelings (or in other words, practicing mindfulness). Increased awareness and acceptance allow us to respond to ourselves and the world around us in a kinder and gentler way, without getting caught up in negative patterns of thought, judgment, and action.

Mindfulness training programs are now in many schools, hospitals, prisons, workplaces, and elsewhere, and there are varying types of programs. Some programs build on the original Mindfulness-Based Stress Reduction (MBSR) program developed by Jon Kabat-Zinn,[1] others focus only on meditation practice, while others still are specifically tailored to distinct groups (for example, teachers, healthcare workers, pregnant women, people suffering from depression and/or anxiety, etc.). There are courses for beginners, courses for more advanced participants, and courses for people who want to become certified trainers.

One of the reasons mindfulness training has become so popular is because research shows it changes our brains and our bodies in positive ways, leading to improvements in physical health, mental health, and well-being. One of the most significant effects is that it increases our ability to *dial down our stress response*, which is a primary focus of the groundbreaking MBSR training. Neuroscience studies have shown that mindfulness interventions impact two stress resilience pathways in the brain. First, they lead to increased activity in the stress regulatory regions of the prefrontal cortex. And second, they lead to decreased activity in the brain's stress alarm system. In other words, mindfulness practice makes us less reactive to and better able to regulate stressors.

Because stress can impair the body's immune system and worsen health problems, it is not surprising that mindfulness also has downstream benefits on mental and physical health. Many high-quality randomized controlled trials (the gold standard in research) have analyzed the impact of mindfulness training on several stress-related outcomes.

Mental Health Benefits of Mindfulness

Studies have shown that mindfulness training and practice help us achieve a state of acceptance, increased focus, and more positive emotions. When you allow yourself to be in the present moment without resistance, you are less likely to ruminate about negative events in the past or worry about the future. A calm and positive emotional state can replace negative thoughts and feelings typically associated with depression, anxiety, and other mental health problems.

For example, Richard Chambers and colleagues evaluated the effects of a 10-day intensive mindfulness meditation training retreat on a non-clinical group of novice meditators. Compared to another group that did not receive the training, they found that participants had significant improvements in working memory and sustained attention and decreases in rumination and depressive symptoms.[2] Other studies have reported similar findings for clinical participants. In a meta-analysis of 39 of these studies, Stefan Hofmann and colleagues found that mindfulness-based therapy was moderately effective for improving anxiety and mood disorders in clinical populations, labeling it a "promising" intervention.[3] They concluded that this approach is useful for changing cognitive and affective processes that underlie multiple clinical issues.

Mindfulness training seems to help us accentuate the positive and minimize the negative, in turn allowing us to enjoy our positive feelings and focus less on what upsets us while promoting our mental health. This effect has been found even for very brief mindfulness interventions. For example, Shannon Erisman and Lizabeth Roemer looked at the effects of a brief mindfulness intervention on participants' responses to film clips that contained either positive or mixed emotions. Compared to participants in the group who didn't receive the training, participants reported higher levels of positive emotions after the positive film clip and less negative emotions after watching the affectively mixed clips.[4]

The role of mindfulness in improving mental health has received mainstream acceptance. Sources such as WebMD tout the benefits of mindfulness for mental health:

> Mindfulness helps you become more aware of what's happening in the present moment and to understand your thought patterns. It allows you to step out of your mind and observe those patterns. This way, you can notice when you are drifting into a mental health problem. When you practice mindfulness, it gets easy to identify stress, anxiety or depression signals early on. You become more positive in the way you respond to signs of mental health problems. It's like making peace with your body by listening and responding to each sensation you experience.[5]

Physical Health Benefits of Mindfulness

Not only does mindfulness training impact our emotional adjustment and mental health, but it also impacts our minds and bodies, particularly with stress-related disease-specific outcomes. These effects are most pronounced in high-stress groups, where stress is partly responsible for the beginning of disease or for making it worse. People who live under stressful conditions (e.g., unemployment, chronic poverty, trauma exposure, etc.) will be most positively impacted by mindfulness training. And the effects are likely to be strongest for diseases where stress fosters onset or causes the disease to get worse.

Think for a minute about diseases most linked to stress. What comes to mind? Clearly, post-traumatic stress disorder (PTSD) is a prime candidate. Most of us would think of heart disease as well, a leading killer in the United States and elsewhere. But you should also realize that many other conditions and diseases are linked to stress, including chronic pain, rheumatoid arthritis, psoriasis, HIV progression, irritable bowel syndrome (IBS), fibromyalgia, and even cancer.

Remember, stress suppresses the effectiveness of our immune system, thereby impacting our ability to resist and fight off disease. Specifically, people who consistently experience high stress levels can develop a reduced sensitivity to cortisol, which normally regulates and turns off the immune response. This insensitivity to cortisol then leads to a "toxic" immune environment and triggers chronic inflammation, which contributes to various diseases.

Recent reviews of well-controlled, randomized studies looking at mindfulness training and physical health have found positive effects of training on many disease-specific outcomes.[6]

These include:

- Improved pain management for patients with lower back pain, rheumatoid arthritis, and fibromyalgia.
- Acceleration of treatment-related skin clearing in psoriasis patients.
- Decreases in IBS symptoms.
- Decreases in susceptibility to colds.
- Decreases in insulin resistance and fasting glucose among people at risk for type 2 diabetes.

There also is increasing support for the benefits of mindfulness training for the prevention of disease and disorder. For example, the American Heart Association released a scientific statement based on their review of available studies. They concluded that taken as a whole, research studies suggest a possible benefit of meditation on reducing cardiovascular risk.[7] Mindfulness training may even prevent some of the cognitive decline associated with aging, and it can even lead to improvement in cognitive functioning in people with Alzheimer's. In a review of research studies with older populations, Tim Gard and colleagues concluded that "meditation interventions for older adults are feasible, and preliminary evidence suggests that meditation can offset age-related cognitive decline."[8]

The Benefits of Gratitude

Gratitude is easy to define and simple to practice. All you need to do is count your blessings, take notice of good things, stop to appreciate what is good in your life, and focus on what you have instead of what you don't have. Yet, we often find it easier to focus on the negative rather than the positive. That's because we are hardwired to attend to negative stimuli more readily than positive stimuli and fixate and dwell on what's wrong longer than we reflect on what's right. Put simply: Bad stuff hits us harder and sticks longer.

This just means that we must work more at practicing gratitude. We must be more intentional to refocus on the goodness in our lives. No matter how many challenges we face, there is something to be thankful for each day. Practicing gratitude doesn't require taking a course, developing a new skill, or spending any money. We all have the ability and opportunity to cultivate it. (See Chapter 5 for some helpful tips.) Gratitude practice helps us train our brain to be aware of and appreciate all of our blessings. It has surged in popularity as a quick and easy strategy for improving our mental health, physical health, and social connections.

Mental Health Benefits of Gratitude

Why do you think gratitude might benefit your mental health? That's simple. Gratitude generates positive emotions and makes us happier and more resilient to stress. Sounds much like one of the benefits of mindfulness, although the process is a little different. Mindfulness wards off negative judgments about our present experience, whereas gratitude fills our hearts and minds with positive thoughts and emotions about the past, present, and future, literally leaving less room for darkness and negativity.

In a landmark study on the effects of gratitude practice, Robert Emmons and Michael McCullough randomly assigned participants to one of three groups. The first group was told to write a few sentences each week about things they were grateful for. The second group was told to write about daily irritations or bad things that happened to them. The third group was told to write about events more generally (without any emphasis on whether they were positive or negative). As you might guess, the group that wrote about gratitude reported feeling better about their lives and being more optimistic about the future. This should come as no surprise. After all, if you feel your current life has an abundance of good things, you will not only feel good about it, but you should also expect more of the same in the future.[9]

Practicing gratitude also makes us feel better about ourselves and less resentful of others. Rather than comparing yourself to someone else and looking for how that person is better than you—a blow to your self-esteem—focusing on what is good in your life makes you feel better about yourself. And the more you feel good about yourself, the less likely you are to compare yourself to others.

People who feel better about their lives and look to the future with hope and optimism are less likely to experience depression, anxiety, and the negative effects of stressors. In a large study conducted by Kenneth Kendler and colleagues, people who practice being thankful experienced significantly lower risk for major depression, generalized anxiety disorder, phobias, nicotine and alcohol dependence, and drug abuse.[10] When you are grateful, the feel-good chemicals in your brain are released, helping to prevent mental health issues like depression and anxiety. If you have positive and grateful thoughts rather than negative ruminations running through your head when you go to sleep, you're also more likely to sleep more soundly.[11] And good sleep is critical for both our mental and physical health.

Physical Health Benefits of Gratitude

Gratitude promotes physical health and well-being. In addition to improved sleep quality, studies show that gratitude is linked to fewer physical symptoms and physical pain, reports of increased daily vitality and energy, and reductions in hypertension.[12] These findings are the same for people who are predisposed to be grateful (in other words, those with a grateful disposition) and those who receive training in gratitude practice.

Why would gratitude predict better physical health? As we mentioned earlier, gratitude leads to positive emotions, which in turn is linked to improvements in both mental health and physical health. Remember the saying, laughter is the best medicine? It's true. Positive emotions are good for your health! They are associated with both prevention of disease and improved recovery following disease. For example, in one study, elderly cardiovascular patients who reported greater positive emotions and

Figure 3.2 Nancy's mother on her 101st birthday. Living a life of gratitude and good health.
Source: © Nancy Guerra and Kirk R. Williams

happiness for 90 days after hospital release had lower readmission rates to the hospital, with effects being even stronger for factors like health status at release or length of stay in the hospital.[13]

In addition to the benefits of positive affect, gratitude practice is also linked to a healthier lifestyle. People who are more grateful are more likely to stay active, eat healthy foods, have a strong social support network, and seek help for medical conditions. An explanation of these factors is likely found in the link between gratitude and self-control. Feeling grateful can help you slow down, not act impulsively, make better decisions, and appreciate and care for your body. It makes sense, then, that gratitude would be associated with healthier lifestyle behaviors like exercise, good nutrition, and going to the doctor.[14]

Gratitude and Relationships

Imagine you drove two hours in traffic to pick up your friend from the airport. As you were driving back, she told you all about her vacation, where she was planning to go next, and how anxious she was to get home. But she never said thank you for picking her up. How would you react? At the very least, we expect you wouldn't go out of your way again to pick her up. That's because humans like doing things for people who are grateful—and we often *dislike* doing things for those who are ungrateful.

Gratitude improves the quality of personal relationships. If we are grateful for what our friend or partner has done for us, we are more likely to reciprocate the action, which in turn improves the quality of

Figure 3.3 Snow angels. We always take time to show affection towards each other—and have fun!
Source: © Nancy Guerra and Kirk R. Williams

our relationship and helps us focus on what is good in our relationships. This upward spiral of showing gratitude seems particularly important in intimate relationships. Showing gratitude to those we love is a great way to make the relationship better.

Expressing gratitude also helps us work through challenges and difficulties in both friendships and intimate relationships.

For example, Nathaniel Lambert and Frank Fincham found that expressing gratitude in relationships was positively associated with comfort in voicing relationship concerns and having a more positive perception of one's partner.[15] It might be that we feel more comfortable discussing challenges within the context of regular reminders of the benefits and strengths of our relationships (that is, what our friends and partners appreciate about us and what we appreciate about them).

Try expressing gratitude with someone you care about. Spend a day or a week being thankful for all the good things about your relationship without mentioning anything that bothers you. Take mental notes of how this person reacts to you. Expressing gratitude is a compelling way to show affection and signal how much we care about our partner. And isn't that the foundation of a solid relationship?

The Benefits of Kindness and Altruism

As we discuss in more detail in Chapter 5, kindness and altruism are distinct virtues related to compassion. Kindness involves being friendly, generous, and considerate—but it does not necessarily involve being helpful to others, which is a key component of altruism. For example, giving someone a compliment is kind, but not altruistic. Most all altruistic acts would be considered kind, except things like donating to a charity to achieve social status rather than to help others.

You probably have heard of the random acts of kindness model of doing kind deeds when not expected. Such acts involve doing something to help or positively affect someone "just because." Most random acts of kindness involve helping others, typically people we don't know. Altruism also involves helping others without focusing on benefits (or even costs) to the self. In practice, relevant research focuses primarily on the benefits of helping more generally, whether it is called kindness or altruism.

Earlier in this chapter, we mentioned the "helper's high." Think about a recent example of something you did that was kind and helpful to someone else, whether it be someone you knew well or a stranger. How did you feel after? Chances are you felt energized and exhilarated, then calm and serene. Again, this feeling is known as the helper's high. Research has shown that this is more than just a feeling. It is accompanied by positive changes in your body's immune system and a lower level of stress hormones.

But how does this physiological response work? Simply put, when you do something to help others, the part of your brain known as the reward reinforcement system is activated, releasing feel-good transmitters such as oxytocin and vasopressin. Consequently, you feel good and are more likely to help in the future. This applies even if you only *are thinking* about helping others. If we think about this from an evolutionary perspective (as we discussed in Chapter 2), then our survival depends on our interdependence. So, it makes sense that we are wired to receive pleasure when we do something that benefits others.

In addition to feelings of immediate pleasure, research has demonstrated how helping benefits our mental and physical health.

Benefits of Kindness and Gratitude on Mental Health, Physical Health, and Overall Well-Being

Most research on the effects of kindness, altruism, and helping behaviors has looked broadly at the effects on well-being, including mental health, physical health, positive feelings, stress relief, social connectedness, and longevity.

Similar to practicing mindfulness and gratitude, helping behaviors activate areas of the brain associated with positive feelings. As we mentioned earlier, positive affect helps prevent mental health issues such as anxiety and depression and simultaneously promotes well-being. Positive affect helps us approach challenges with confidence, expand our social networks, and prepare for future tasks with optimism and hope. It boosts our immune system and helps us moderate our stress reactivity.

Studies find that performing acts of kindness and helping, even small acts like petting an animal or bringing someone a cup of coffee, boost our happiness and well-being. They also boost our physical health. For example, well-known positive psychologist Sonja Lyubomirsky and colleagues found that people who performed different acts of kindness, anything that involved helping, sharing, or caring for someone, showed improvements in gene expression associated with a healthier immune system. This suggests one potential mechanism to explain the physical health benefits of helping.[16] Disease resistance, in turn, contributes to increases in longevity.

The role of helping behavior in health and longevity was also studied by Sonja Hilbrand and colleagues. In a prospective study of older adults in Germany (the Berlin Aging Study), they found that supporting others, including active grandparenting, predicted both better health and enhanced longevity.[17] In another study with over 7,000 US adults, Eric Kim and Sara Konrath found that people who volunteered regularly engaged in more preventive health behaviors (for example, flu shots and regular lab testing) than those who did not.[18]

Figure 3.4 Global Service Scholars program in Peru.
Source: © Nancy Guerra and Kirk R. Williams

We have focused on how being kind and helping others affects us. But keep in mind that we also must extend kindness and helping *towards ourselves*, as doing so leads to enormous benefits for our health and well-being. As we will explore in Chapter 6, kindness is a cornerstone of self-compassion. Indeed, being good to yourself, treating yourself with loving kindness, and engaging in self-help behaviors are critical for your mental and physical health. Higher levels of self-compassion have been associated with a range of positive outcomes including increased feelings of well-being and decreased anxiety, depression, rumination, and fear of failure.[19]

A Compassion-Driven Life Promotes Well-Being

Compassion and related virtues bring us happiness and pleasure, lower our stress levels, increase our connections with others, promote health and well-being, and may even help us live longer. And all these benefits are interconnected. When we do something that makes us feel positive about ourselves and others, we are less likely to fixate on negative events and better able to manage stressors. And as we know, stress impairs the body's immune system and makes us more susceptible to disease. On the other hand, happiness, when linked to purpose and meaning in life (when we help others or work for a cause), predicts lower levels of inflammation, a root cause of many diseases.

More and more research studies demonstrate the benefits of compassion for health and well-being. We believe that compassion practice should be considered just as important as healthy eating, exercise, preventive screenings, and other routine practices for promoting and increasing our quality of life. It should be regularly encouraged in schools, the workplace, healthcare, and beyond.

Notes

1   Kabat-Zinn, J. (2003). Mindfulness-based stress reduction. *Constructivism in the Human Sciences, 8* (2), 73–83.
2   Chambers, R., Chuen Yee Lo, & Allen, N. (2008). The impact of intensive mindfulness training on attentional control, cognitive style, and affect. *Cognitive therapy and research, 32*, 303–322.
3   Hoffmann, S. G., Sawyer, A. T., Witt, A. A., & Oh, D. (2010). The effect of mindfulness-based therapy on anxiety and depression: A meta-analytic review. *Journal of Consulting and Clinical Psychology, 78*, 169–183. DOI: 10.1037/a0018555.

4   Erisman. S. M. & Roemer, L. (2010). A preliminary investigation of the effects of experimentally induced mindfulness on emotional responding to film clips. *Emotion*, *10*, 72–82. DOI: 10.1037/a0017162.

5   WebMD, www.webmd.com/balance/stress-management/what-to-know-about-mindfulness-and-mental-health

6   Creswell, J. D., Lindsay, E. K., Villalba D. K., & Chin, B. (2019). Mindfulness training and physical health: Mechanisms and outcomes. *Psychosomatic Medicine*, *81*, 224–232. DOI: 10.1098/PSY0000000000000675.

7   Levine, G. N. et al. (2017). Meditation and cardiovascular risk reduction. *Journal of the American Heart Association*, 6: e002218.

8   Gard, T., Holzel, B., & Lazar, S. W. (2014). The potential effects of meditation on age-related cognitive decline: A systematic review. *Annals of the New York Academy of Sciences*, *1307*. DOI:10.1111/nyas.12348.

9   Emmons, R. A. & McCullough, M. E. (2003). Counting blessings versus burdens: An experimental investigation of gratitude and subjective well-being in daily life. *Journal of Personality and Social Psychology*, *84*, 377–389.

10 Kendler, K. S., Liu, X., Gardner, C. O., McCullough, M. E., Larson, D., & Prescott, C. (2003). Dimensions of religiosity and their relationship to lifetime psychiatric and substance use disorders. *American Journal of Psychiatry*, *160*, 496–503.

11 Wood, A. M., Joseph, S., Lloyd, J., & Atkins. S. (2009). Gratitude influences sleep through the mechanism of pre-sleep cognitions. *Journal of Psychosomatic Research*, *66*, 43–48.

12 Emmons, R. A. & McCullough, M. E. (2003). Counting blessings versus burdens: An experimental investigation of gratitude and subjective well-being in daily life. *Journal of Personality and Social Psychology*, *84*, 377–389.

13 Middleton, R. A. & Byrd, E. K. (1996). Psychosocial factors and hospital readmission status of older persons with cardiovascular disease. *Journal of Applied Rehabilitation Counseling*, *27* (4), 3–10.

14 Hill, P. L., Allemand, M., & Roberts, B. W. (2013). Examining the pathways between gratitude and self-rated physical health across adulthood. *Personality and Individual Differences*, *54*, 92–96.

15 Lambert, N. M. & Fincham, F. D. (2011). Expressing gratitude to a partner leads to more relationship maintenance behavior. *Emotion*, *11* (1), 52–60. https://doi.org/10.1037/a0021557

16 Nelson-Coffey, K. S., Fritz, M. M., Lyubormirsky, S., and Cole, S. W. (2017) Kindness in the blood: A randomized controlled trial of the gene regulatory impact of prosocial behavior. *Psychneuroendocrinology*, *81*, 8–13.

17 Hilbrand, S., Coall, D.A., Meyer, A. H., Gerstorf, D., & Hertwig, R. (2017). A prospective study of associations among helping, health and longevity. *Social Science Medicine*, *187*, 109–117. DOI: 10.1016/j.socscimed.2017.06.035.

18 Kim, E. S. & Konrath, S. H. (2016). Volunteering is prospectively associated with health care use among older adults. *Social Science & Medicine*, *149*, 122–129.

19 Neff, K. (2009). Self-compassion. In M. R. Leary & R. H. Hoyle (eds), *Handbook of individual differences in social behavior*. Guilford Press, pp. 561–563.

References

WebMD, www.webmd.com/balance/stress-management/what-to-know-about-mindfulness-and-mental-health

Chambers, R., Chuen Yee Lo, & Allen, N. (2008). The impact of intensive mindfulness training on attentional control, cognitive style, and affect. *Cognitive therapy and research*, *32*, 303–322.

Creswell, J. D., Lindsay, E. K., Villalba D. K., & Chin, B. (2019). Mindfulness training and physical health: Mechanisms and outcomes. *Psychosomatic Medicine, 81*, 224–232. DOI: 10.1098/PSY0000000000000675.

Emmons, R. A. & McCullough, M. E. (2003). Counting blessings versus burdens: An experimental investigation of gratitude and subjective well-being in daily life. *Journal of Personality and Social Psychology, 84*, 377–389.

Erisman. S. M. & Roemer, L. (2010). A preliminary investigation of the effects of experimentally induced mindfulness on emotional responding to film clips. *Emotion, 10*, 72–82. DOI: 10.1037/a0017162.

Gard, T., Holzel, B., & Lazar, S. W. (2014). The potential effects of meditation on age-related cognitive decline: A systematic review. *Annals of the New York Academy of Sciences, 1307*. DOI:10.1111/nyas.12348.

Hilbrand, S., Coall, D. A., Meyer, A. H., Gerstorf, D., & Hertwig, R. (2017). A prospective study of associations among helping, health and longevity. *Social Science Medicine, 187*, 109–117. DOI: 10.1016/j.socscimed.2017.06.035.

Hill, P. L., Allemand, M., & Roberts, B. W. (2013). Examining the pathways between gratitude and self-rated physical health across adulthood. *Personality and Individual Differences, 54*, 92–96.

Hoffmann, S. G., Sawyer, A. T., Witt, A. A., & Oh, D. (2010). The effect of mindfulness-based therapy on anxiety and depression: A meta-analytic review. *Journal of Consulting and Clinical Psychology, 78*, 169–83. DOI: 10.1037/a0018555.

Kabat-Zinn, J. (2003). Mindfulness-based stress reduction. *Constructivism in the Human Sciences, 8*(2), 73–83.

Kendler, K. S., Liu, X., Gardner, C. O., McCullough, M. E., Larson, D., & Prescott, C. (2003). Dimensions of religiosity and their relationship to lifetime psychiatric and substance use disorders. *American Journal of Psychiatry, 160*, 496–503.

Kim, E. S., & Konrath, S. H. (2016). Volunteering is prospectively associated with health care use among older adults. *Social Science & Medicine, 149*, 122–129.

Lambert, N. M. & Fincham, F. D. (2011). Expressing gratitude to a partner leads to more relationship maintenance behavior. Emotion, 11(1), 52–60. https://doi.org/10.1037/a0021557

Levine, G. N. et al. (2017). Meditation and cardiovascular risk reduction. *Journal of the American Heart Association*, 6: e002218.

Middleton, R. A. & Byrd, E. K. (1996). Psychosocial factors and hospital readmission status of older persons with cardiovascular disease. *Journal of Applied Rehabilitation Counseling, 27*(4), 3–10.

Neff, K. (2009). Self-compassion. In M. R. Leary & R. H. Hoyle (eds), *Handbook of individual differences in social behavior.* The Guilford Press, pp. 561–563.

Nelson-Coffey, K. S., Fritz, M. M., Lyubormirsky, S., and Cole, S. W. (2017). Kindness in the blood: A randomized controlled trial of the gene regulatory impact of prosocial behavior. *Psychneuroendocrinology, 81*, 8–13.

Wood, A. M., Joseph, S., Lloyd, J., & Atkins, S. (2009). Gratitude influences sleep through the mechanism of pre-sleep cognitions. *Journal of Psychosomatic Research, 66*, 43–48.

PART II
THE HOW OF COMPASSION

4

GETTING STARTED

DECLUTTERING, REFRAMING, AND SETTING YOUR INTENTION

Now that you've read about the *what* and the *why* of compassion, it's time to turn to the *how*. The first thing we need to do is to make space for compassion. What do you think this means? How do you think you can do this? We'll discuss three specific techniques that will facilitate making space for compassion and thus prepare us for a lifelong compassionate journey.

Technique 1: Decluttering Your Physical Space

The first technique to think about is decluttering. It's a great place to start, and here's why. Clutter is chaotic; it breeds tension, unease, and anxiety. It distracts you and interferes with your ability to focus. It is the opposite of synchrony and harmony.

We live in a world that is getting more cluttered by the day. There are countless choices in the supermarket. Think about how many varieties of yogurt or ice cream or cereal you have to sift through before you put something in your cart. Pumping gas, you are bombarded with music, videos, and car wash decisions. Think about clutter in your digital space. How many unread emails do you have in your inbox? How many people are waiting for you to answer a text? How many advertisements pop up when you are online? How many devices do you have vying for your attention?

DOI: 10.4324/9781003312437-6

Let's look at the clutter in your personal life next, starting with where you are sitting or standing right now. Take a few moments to look at the physical objects around you. Does your space feel crowded, even frenetic, with objects strewn about? Or is your space organized and tidy? Do the colors and textures feel soothing? Do you get a sense of peace, comfort, and tranquility when you look around? Or do you feel like you are in an asteroid field?

You might think that clutter in your physical space doesn't matter, that you can focus and be your best anywhere. But that's not what research shows. For example, in one recent study of nearly 1,500 adults aged 18 and older, clutter in the home was negatively related to well-being, contributing to feelings of personal dissatisfaction and alienation.[1] Another study found that mothers who lived in cluttered environments had higher levels of the stress hormone cortisol compared to mothers who lived in more restful, less chaotic environments.[2]

In other words, *mess equals stress.* And stress translates to poor lifestyle choices, which lead to poorer physical health outcomes. Did you know that living in a cluttered home, or even just being in a cluttered room, makes you more likely to make unhealthy food choices? It's true. People in cluttered homes are more likely to be overweight, and just being in a messy room can make you more likely to eat a candy bar than a piece of fruit.[3]

Your brain is wired to keep track of only a few details for a short period of time, and it can get overloaded when there is too much going on. It's

Figure 4.1 A beautiful mountain lake radiates peace and serenity. Nature calms and heals us.
Source: © Nancy Guerra and Kirk R. Williams

even more difficult to process what you see in a cluttered environment. In one recent study, viewers found it harder to interpret emotional expressions of characters in movie scenes when the background was highly cluttered.[4] That means it's harder to figure out what people are feeling when they are in a cluttered space.

Clutter in your physical space affects how much you are willing to help others. In fact, just being in an orderly room makes you more likely to donate money to charity. In another interesting experiment, college students were assigned to either a neat and orderly room or a messy and cluttered room. The students were presented with a series of tasks and then asked whether they wanted to donate the money they received for participating in the study to a charity. Findings showed that participants in the orderly room donated more than twice as much money as those in the messy room.[5]

But clutter isn't limited to our physical space. We also clutter our minds. Do you frequently have the same incessant thoughts that stick around like a bad cold? Do you ever have trouble going to sleep because you can't stop thinking? Do you replay a troubling scene over and over in your mind? Do you dwell on things that are bad and harmful for a long time? If so, you've experienced *rumination*, which is defined by psychologists as a mode of responding to distress that entails repetitively and passively focusing on distress and its possible causes and consequences. Rumination pretty much is limited to bad things, thus increasing our stress and anxiety and interfering with our happiness and well-being.

Perhaps you have so many thoughts running through your head that you find it difficult to focus on what you are doing. How often does that happen? Every day? Several times a day? Indeed, psychologists have a term for this mental chatter. It's called *mind wandering*, defined as "thoughts not tied to the immediate environment; thoughts that shift away from the task at hand."[6]

If this describes you, fear not, for you are far from alone. You may be surprised to learn that 96% of adults in the United States say they experience mind wandering daily and that it occupies as much as 50% of their waking hours. This is not just a concern in the United States. A global study involving 5,000 people from 83 countries yielded the conclusion that mind wandering is the brain's "default mode of operation."[7]

Now, mind wandering isn't always bad. Sometimes we must be able to think about more than one thing at a time. Sometimes mind wandering can lead to creative ideas and new ways of thinking. But more often than not, mind wandering has a toxic component to it. We tend to think mainly about ourselves and our problems. Too much mind wandering can even interfere with our happiness.

The negative effects of this physical and mental clutter are so profound that a cottage industry in decluttering advice has emerged from a broad assortment of books and life coaches. There are decluttering workbooks, no-nonsense guides to decluttering, and best-selling books about how to declutter. There are books, websites, and training programs about decluttering your mind. Before you buy these or sign up for a program, take a moment to fill out the self-assessment below.

Following this, we provide some quick and easy tips for decluttering. If your score is pretty high (let's say over 20) you might want to take a deeper dive and look for some extra help.

<u>YOUR TURN</u>: Rate the clutter in your life on a 1–10 point scale.

THE PLACES I LIVE AND WORK ARE CLUTTERED AND DISTRACTING.

1	2	3	4	5	6	7	8	9	10
Not at all				Somewhat				A lot	

I RUMINATE ABOUT THINGS THAT BOTHER ME.

1	2	3	4	5	6	7	8	9	10
Not at all				Somewhat				A lot	

MY MIND CONSTANTLY IS WANDERING.

1	2	3	4	5	6	7	8	9	10
Not at all				Somewhat				A lot	

Helpful Tips for Decluttering Your Physical Space

Here are some strategies for decluttering your physical space.

- *Make a commitment.* Believe in yourself. Make up your mind to create and maintain more calm and serene physical spaces.
- *Use your imagination.* What do you want the spaces around you to look like? Look online or in magazines to find pictures of spaces

you like—spaces that are calming for you. Imagine your perfect lifestyle in a single picture or photo. What does it look like?

- *Take stock.* Look at all the objects around you. Which are particularly useful? Which are not? Which items make you happy and joyful? What can you pack up or give away? Focus only on what you want to keep. Make a list of what you want to keep and why.

- *Make a plan and take action.* Write down an action plan before you start. Most experts recommend that you first get rid of things that are not meaningful or useful. You can sell these items, donate them, give them away, or throw them out. After that, move on to organizing what you are keeping. Do this by types of items—for instance, organize your clothes, your pots and pans, etc. Set aside an entire day (or more) to declutter so you can quickly see results.

- *Make decluttering part of your daily routine.* Decluttering is more than just a one-time action. Think of some rules you can follow that will prevent clutter from coming back. For example, never put anything away twice. If you bring home a bag of clothes, don't drop the bag on the floor with the thought that you'll put the clothes away tomorrow. Bring the bag in and put the clothes away immediately.

Helpful Tips for Decluttering Your Mind

Next, let's turn to some strategies for decluttering your *mind*.

- *Start by quieting your mind.* When you are physically tired, you'll likely try to get some rest. But when is the last time you rested your mind? And we don't mean distracting your mind with television,

Figure 4.2 Symmetry provides a feeling of calmness, harmony, and tranquility. Jaipur, India.
Source: © Nancy Guerra and Kirk R. Williams

video games, reading, or other activities. We mean keeping your mind still—like a calm lake at sunset. An easy technique is to find a quiet setting without distractions, and slowly and attentively *breathe in through your nose and out through your mouth*, repeating several times until you feel your mind becoming more restful. If it helps, you can visualize your thoughts as clouds passing by in the sky, appearing and disappearing in a slow rhythm.

- *Focus your mind through directed attention.* Once you have calmed your mind, try focusing with deliberate attention. After you find a comfortable breathing rhythm, one strategy is to start counting your breath from 1 to 10, and then start again. Or focus your attention by mentally noting in-breaths and out-breaths. Catch yourself when you are distracted, when your mind wanders, and gently bring it back. Refocusing on your breathing is helpful. You can also focus your attention on an image, like a candle burning a few feet in front of you.

- *Strengthening awareness.* Another strategy for decluttering your mind is to practice present-moment awareness. Begin with deep, regular breaths, then notice what is going on around you: any sounds, sights, or feelings you are experiencing. Simply view yourself as if you were an observer rather than an actor. Or, next time you're out in nature or just taking in the birds, the trees, and the sky above you, try focusing your awareness on what you are doing. Let go of this focused awareness and simply observe whatever else you are experiencing: thoughts, feelings, discomfort, or whatever comes and goes.

Technique 2: Reframing

We are what we think. All that we are arises with our thoughts. With our thoughts we make the world. Speak or act with a pure mind and happiness will follow you, as your shadow, unbreakable.

In a nutshell, this famous quote from Buddha means that we create our world through our thoughts. Of course, there are external realities we can't just wish away with our thoughts, such as unbearable heat, heavy traffic, illness, or financial hardship. Nonetheless, how you interpret, understand, and react to these (and other) experiences depends, in part, on your own thinking. You must *frame* these events so they make sense to you—so they fit in with your worldview and give you a guide for action.

Your cognitive frame is like a pair of glasses that illuminates how you view any given situation. The glasses can help you see things more clearly, or they can distort your experiences. What does it mean to say that someone sees the world through rose-colored glasses? Did you know this idiom dates back to the mid-1800s? It refers to someone who has an upbeat, hopeful, and optimistic style of thinking—someone who always looks on the bright side or sees the silver lining (or the rose color) when things go wrong.

What kind of glasses are you wearing? Do you tend to look for the good in everything (or at least realize that even failures are opportunities to learn and do better next time)? Or do you find yourself frequently trapped in a mode of negative, anxious, unproductive thinking, focusing on what's wrong instead of what's right? Do you think that others are generally self-centered and uncaring, or do you experience the world as a joyful place where people care about each other and about doing the right thing? As you can imagine, someone who sees the world as a dangerous and unhappy place is more likely to relate to others out of fear, suspicion, rivalry, and even hatred, whereas someone with a more positive attitude is more likely to relate to others out of kindness and compassion. A positive lens really can set the stage for compassion.

Your cognitive frame is both global and specific. By *global*, we mean a general orientation—like optimism or pessimism—that acts like a lens through which you interpret situations. Your cognitive frame also includes more *specific* beliefs about people, places, objects, and events. As we mentioned earlier, your brain is only wired to keep track of a few details for a short period of time, and it can get overloaded when there is too much going on. Your brain doesn't like mental clutter, so it develops a set of cognitive shortcuts or *cognitive schema* to prevent information overload. Although these mental shortcuts are useful (even essential, at times) in helping us process the overwhelming amount of information we encounter, they also can narrow our thinking and cause us to over-look relevant information, misinterpret events, and make biased or stere-otyped judgments.

If you doubt the power of belief, consider the profound impact of *expectation effects*, meaning how expectations influence perceptions and behavior. There is a large body of research demonstrating that specific expectation beliefs shape our responses and outcomes across a broad range of situations. A very simple, well-known, widely used expectation belief studied by the motivational psychologist Carol Dweck is called *mindset*. Related most closely to academic and career success, she has identified and studied the impact of two basic types of mindsets: a *fixed mindset* and a *growth mindset*. People with a fixed mindset see their abilities as something they are born with and cannot change. People with a growth mindset believe they can improve at what they are doing through effort. Many studies have linked a growth mindset to academic and career success, in some cases showing that it matters even more than socioeconomic background.[8]

Another interesting example of the power of expectation effects comes from research on *placebos* and *nocebos*. (A nocebo is, simply put, the opposite of a placebo.) A placebo effect occurs when your expectation of a positive outcome results in a positive outcome; for instance, when a sugar pill you are told should give you energy actually predicts an increase in your energy, including changes in biological markers. A nocebo effect is when your expectation of a negative outcome results in a negative outcome; for instance, if you are told something will really hurt, you are more likely to experience it as painful than if you are not given that information. Studies across a range of situations have demonstrated robust placebo and nocebo effects, suggesting that our expectations of what will happen help predict what does happen.[9] As the famous American sociologists W.I. Thomas and Dorothy Swaine Thomas said, "If men define situations as real, they are real in their consequences."[10]

Before we talk more about how our mental schema and beliefs can promote or interfere with compassion, let us reiterate that they serve a critical role in simplifying the massive amount of information we process from moment to moment. They are particularly important when we must make quick decisions, such as responding to threat or danger. Whether these schema or beliefs come from deep-rooted cognitive frames (such as our mindset) or are the product of situational manipulations (such as placebo and nocebo effects), they clearly impact how we understand and react to a range of situations. They are essential and often helpful—but they also can crowd our mental space and interfere with compassion.

Think about a belief you hold that might cause you to judge a situation without gathering enough information to know why it happened. Most everyone jumps to conclusions at least once in a while, particularly under conditions of ambiguity or potential danger. However, if you do this regularly, it can interfere with your ability to demonstrate compassion.

For whatever reason, we are hardwired to attend more quickly to *negative* than positive stimuli. When we feel threatened or uncertain about a situation, our tendency is to assume the worst. Our tendency to focus on the negative over the positive also leads to a more general *negativity bias*. Negative, or adverse, events have a more significant impact on us than positive events. This is even more challenging to recognize when our negative biases operate at a subconscious level, leading to an *unconscious* or *implicit bias*. We all have some unconscious biases, which typically interfere with compassion.

The good news is that we can redirect our thought processes to promote compassion. Doing so requires sustained practice, but it pays off in sustained rewards. As Thupten Jinpa said in *A Fearless Heart*, "By changing the way we perceive ourselves and the world we live in, we can transform the way we experience ourselves and the world"(loc 1109).[11] In short, by changing how we think, we can change our lives and the lives of others for the better.

Let us now spend a few moments considering how we can increase our awareness of and *reframe* our thinking to facilitate compassion. We'll consider the reasons behind and strategies to change three specific cognitive shortcuts: *jumping to conclusions, focusing on the negative*, and *implicit bias*.

Jumping to Conclusions

When you jump to a conclusion, you are using a mental shortcut. While this might help you respond faster, it will also reduce your accuracy. Again, in urgent situations where you must react immediately, this is quite useful. If you see a fire in the forest, you should call 911 before you try to figure out whether it is a forest fire or a controlled burn. Unfortunately, in many other cases, taking a mental shortcut based on limited information will lead you to the wrong conclusion. Rather than experiencing the moment in a nonjudgmental manner, you short-circuit the process and rely on a pre-existing assumption or judgment. This often results in an incorrect assumption or judgment.

Think about the last time you jumped to the wrong conclusion. What were the circumstances? What cues were you responding to? What preconceived notions colored your thinking? Let's look at some common situations in which people jump to conclusions. Take note of the first explanation that comes to your mind as to why each situation occurred.

- Someone cuts you off on the freeway.
- A friend rolls her eyes when you mention a particular person.
- A supervisor at work shuts his door when you walk by.
- Your partner is two hours late to pick you up for dinner and didn't let you know.
- Your friend backs out of an event a few minutes before it starts and says she doesn't feel well.
- You said, "Good morning, how are you?" in a friendly way to an acquaintance and he just said "hey" back without even smiling.

We could go on and on with our list. You probably have many other examples of situations where you jumped to a conclusion. And, given our brain's natural negativity bias, we generally jump to *negative* conclusions. That is, we tend to assume hostile intent or disrespect, and we generally take things personally even if they weren't. *Someone cut me off because they were rude. My supervisor shut his door because he doesn't like me. My friend said she didn't feel well but she really just didn't want to go with me.* Rather than setting the stage for compassion, these negative conclusions set the stage for anger, frustration, hostility, and revenge.

Next, let's think about how you can avoid this rush to judgment.

Helpful Tips to Avoid Jumping to Conclusions

Remember that sometimes it is adaptive and necessary to jump to a conclusion, such as when you are in imminent danger. Most of the time, however, we can avoid rushing to judgment. Here are some useful strategies.

- *Start by slowing down.* Ask yourself whether you need to respond immediately or whether you can allow yourself to be present in the moment, absorbing what you see, feel, hear, or think. Take time to figure things out.

- *Don't assume negative intent.* Don't attribute an action to causes such as malice, disrespect, or incompetence if there is another reasonable explanation. (This point is also known as the aphorism *Hanlon's razor.*)
- *Seek out any additional information you deem relevant.* For example, if someone gives you a harsh look, ask them what's wrong instead of assuming they are mad at you or don't like you. Don't judge people based on stereotypes or unconscious biases. Instead, focus on the facts.
- *Practice perspective taking and empathy (more on this in the next chapter).* Visualize the situation from the other person's perspective. Try to understand what they are thinking and/or try to feel what they are feeling. If you can't place yourself in their shoes, *ask them* how they are feeling. Really *listen* to their answer.
- *Be aware of (and don't commit) the fundamental attribution error.* This is a cognitive bias that causes us to overestimate the influence of individual factors and to underestimate the influence of situational factors on people's behavior. In terms of compassion, this would lead us to blame individuals for their own suffering rather than attribute the cause to external, situational factors.

Focusing on the Negative

As we mentioned earlier, we all are hardwired to register negative stimuli more and to *fixate and dwell* on these stimuli. For example, studies in behavioral economics have shown that the bad feelings associated with losing $50 are much more intense than the happy feelings of finding $50. News stories about car crashes and murder grab our attention more than stories of kindness and goodwill. We recall and think about insults more than compliments. Memories of unpleasant events also last longer than memories of good events. Bad stuff sticks, and even a little bad often outweighs an abundance of good in our minds.

Not only do negative stimuli live large in our minds, but they also predict negative outcomes. For example, in an experimental test looking at the impact of negative vs. positive information on the side effects of an anti-anxiety medication, researchers framed the exact same information in a negative or positive way. One group of participants was told that approximately 27 out of 100 people *will* experience drowsiness as a side effect, while the other group was told that approximately 73 out of 100 people *will not* experience drowsiness. This is exactly the same statistic framed in two lights: negative and positive. Yet, participants in the group who received negative information reported significantly greater short-term negative side effects than those who received positive information.[12]

Given the unpleasantness of negative events relative to positive events, why do they take up so much of our cognitive and emotional space? The answer is simple when viewed in the context of evolution. To survive, our ancestors had to respond to constant environmental threats. So, focusing on danger before pleasure has long been an adaptive response.

The negativity bias is less adaptive in today's world, but it still has us in its grip. We frequently sabotage ourselves with negative self-talk. The bad things we hear or think about ourselves seem to stick more, in part, because we constantly repeat them to ourselves. Negative self-talk is a habit that sets you up to fail. Do you practice negative self-talk? Do you ever say any of these things to yourself:

I.   I never do anything right.
   • I'm no good at _____.
   • Nobody likes me.
   • I just can't do this.
   • I'm so fat/ugly/stupid/etc.

Figure 4.3 Horses are prey animals—they are attuned to danger and seek comfort from each other. Nancy with two neighborhood horses in Pennsylvania.
Source: © Nancy Guerra and Kirk R. Williams

Negative self-talk is a particularly critical roadblock to self-compassion. As we discuss in Chapter 6, self-compassion involves being warm, kind, and understanding towards yourself when things don't work out (rather than being harsh and self-critical).

Our brains evolved to learn more from negative than positive experiences and to store these negative experiences in enduring neural structures. Unfortunately, neural structures underlying gratitude, empathy, honesty, and other inner strengths are much less likely to spring up on their own. In fact, they require sustained effort and practice to learn and keep. As Rick Hanson notes in his best-selling book, *Hardwiring Happiness*:

> If you keep resting your mind on self-criticism, worries, grumbling about others, hurts, and stress, then your brain will be shaped into greater reactivity, vulnerability to anxiety and depressed mood, a narrow focus on threats and losses, and inclinations toward anger, sadness and guilt. On the other hand, if you keep resting your mind on good events and conditions (someone was nice to you, there's a roof over your head), pleasant feelings, the things you do get done, physical pleasures, and your good intentions and qualities, then over time your brain will take a different shape, one with strength and resilience hardwired into it, as well as a realistically optimistic outlook, a positive mood, and a sense of worth. [13]

Here is what one of our university students said about negative self-talk and how to change it:

> I'm overly critical of my physical appearance, specifically my weight. As a former yoga teacher, I was involved in an industry that celebrated thinness and physical perfection. However, I've recently stopped teaching, become more relaxed with my diet, and gained 15 pounds. I've dealt with body image issues and disordered eating for most of my life, and this recent weight gain has led to a constant barrage of negative self-talk. I think to myself, I'm weak and have no willpower, I'll never lose this

weight, and I'm ugly. I am trying to change this negative self-talk to positive self-talk by reminding myself the following:

- I am strong and my body is strong. It gives me so much, and I'm alive and healthy.
- Weight gain is a minor setback and can be fixed.
- I am beautiful and worthy, regardless of how much I weigh or what I look like.

Think about how you can change your negative self-talk into something more positive.

Helpful Tips for Shifting from a Negative to a Positive Focus

Because we are wired to focus on the negative, shifting to a positive orientation requires a conscious and sustained effort. Here are some strategies you can use:

- *Try to catch yourself when you are focusing on negative rather than positive events. Monitor your self-talk and what you say to others.* Use your mindfulness practice to be more aware of the present moment. Imagine that someone is writing down everything you attend to, think, and say, then highlighting all your negative thoughts with a red highlighter. How much red do you see?
- *Practice cognitive restructuring. When you catch yourself in a negative mindset, practice restructuring or reframing it in a positive light.* Try to find silver linings in the negative. Reframe negative self-talk in a more positive manner. For example, imagine you had a below *average* performance evaluation—a situation most everyone has experienced from time to time. Instead of saying, "I'm so stupid, incompetent, etc.," say, "That's not really like me. I need to think about why I wasn't at my best and use what I've learned to do better. I know I can improve." You're not lying or deceiving yourself— you are simply rewiring your brain with a vision of a better you.
- *Savor positive moments.* Refocusing on the positive requires intentional action. The technique of *savoring* helps you take time to appreciate and take delight in the positive moments in life.

We easily savor a good meal or a great wine, but there are many, many feelings, images, and actions we can add to our positive storehouse. Next time you have one of these experiences, *take* a little more time than usual to enjoy it. Remember to reflect on it and re-experience the joy you felt throughout the next day, week, or month. Build up your reservoir of positive images and feelings.

- *Be attentive to external attempts to manipulate your thoughts and actions.* When you see, hear, or read negative information about people, places, or events, make sure to fact-check or consider alternatives. Be aware that those who have or seek power are aware of negativity bias and use negative information to persuade you against things. Try to focus more on what you *are for* than what you *are against* when making important decisions.

Implicit Bias

Throughout history we have seen differential treatment and unequal opportunities for specific groups of people, including groups defined by race/ethnicity, gender, sexuality, age, income, and so on. This unfair treatment has caused considerable suffering, yet it continues. This is not to say that we haven't made progress. Clearly, we have seen an increasing emphasis on the importance of diversity, equity, and fairness across a broad range of settings in recent years. We're becoming more and more sensitized to the harm and suffering caused by racism, ageism, sexism, and other forms of discrimination, and we've made conscious efforts to alleviate this suffering.

That said, what about the persistent biases that are outside of our conscious awareness? If you take a moment to reflect on your own thinking, can you identify any attitudes, prejudices, or judgments that you unconsciously hold about people or groups? Research has shown that most people hold at least some unconscious or implicit biases that act as cognitive shortcuts, automatically influencing their judgments and perceptions of others. And these biases can even be in direct contradiction to their espoused beliefs and values.

A common example is being more receptive or responsive to familiar-sounding names than those from other cultural groups, even if you greatly value cultural diversity. Another example is prejudging members of certain racial/ethnic groups to be more aggressive and deviant. Indeed, there are dozens of laboratory experiments that have shown implicit racial bias. These include studies where harmless objects are more likely to be classified as weapons in the hands of Black men, studies where participants are faster to identify bad words paired with Black faces than white faces, and studies where white participants perceive Black faces to be angrier than white faces with the same expression.[14]

We've all heard stories of the horrendous implicit bias towards people identified as Black and other people of color, particularly by police and other criminal justice officials. Yet implicit bias operates in many other, subtler ways. For example, in the popular book *Blink*, Malcolm Gladwell notes that on average across the general population, only about 3.9% of men are 6 feet 2 inches or taller. And yet in a random sampling of corporate CEOs, he found that about one-third of CEOs fell into this group. As Gladwell suggests, it is possible that those who hire CEOs have an unconscious belief or implicit bias that successful CEOs should be tall men.[15]

Helpful Tips for Confronting Implicit Bias

Keep in mind that counteracting implicit biases is a lifelong commitment. It takes time and practice. Here are some of the best strategies from several different training programs.

- *Overcome denial.* Even if you are aware of your bias, you may not be aware of the extent and consequences of this bias in your everyday life. Take a personal inventory of common biases (for instance, related to age, gender, SES, race/ethnicity) by thinking about different situations you've been in where potential biases might exist and what happened in those situations. There also are several brief tests you can take online. For instance, a well-known test is the IAT (Implicit Association Test). Keep in *mind* that not all researchers agree on the value of the IAT or its relevance to actual behavior.
- *Be mindful.* When you allow yourself to be present in the moment without judgment, you are less likely to react quickly based on unconscious bias. We talk much more about mindfulness in the next chapter, as it is a critical foundation for compassion.

- *Practice perspective taking.* Perspective taking means seeing the world through someone else's eyes. As we discuss in the next chapter, it is an important virtue linked to compassion. To reduce implicit bias, try to imagine how you would feel if you were treated unfairly based on a *specific* characteristic. Listen to stories of people who have experienced implicit bias, and then try to imagine yourself in their shoes.
- *Slow down.* As we've discussed throughout this chapter, we all jump to conclusions, but these conclusions usually are based on limited information and focus on the negative. Before you reach a conclusion about a person, place, or event, make sure you focus your attention on positive attributes.
- *Avoid overgeneralizations.* Remember that any biases based on group characteristics do not mean that an individual from that group will have those characteristics. For example, reams of studies show that neighborhoods with high rates of poverty also tend to have high rates of crime. That doesn't mean every individual living in an impoverished neighborhood is a criminal. Social and *behavioral* scientists refer to such unwarranted judgments as the *ecological fallacy.* When dealing with an individual, focus on what makes that person unique, what you like about that person, and what you have in common.
- *Interact more with different types of people.* Learn about and get to know people unlike you, from different cultures and different lifestyles. Rather than approaching these experiences with preconceived judgments, allow yourself to be open to new experiences.
- *Check your messaging.* How do you communicate with others in terms of exclusivity or inclusivity? Learn to use statements that embrace inclusivity. Use language that reflects dignity and respect for all. This could include *respecting* people's chosen pronouns.
- *Practice reducing your implicit bias in everyday situations. Track your progress.* As noted above, reducing *implicit* bias is a lifelong process that requires regular and ongoing attention. Remember to also be gentle with yourself as you embark on this journey of unlearning years of thoughts and behaviors. There will be inevitable setbacks that see you fall back into your old mental models. Give yourself some grace, and keep sustaining your efforts until it becomes second nature.

Technique 3: Setting Your Intention

Any time you are trying to reach a specific goal, you are setting an intention. Intentions are active, not passive. They provide you with a way to create and participate in life actively as you see fit. This may sound like motivation, but it is different. Motivation is the reason behind what you do, such as wanting to be successful or famous or make the world a better place. Sometimes, we aren't even consciously aware of what motivates us. In contrast, intentions are deliberate. They allow you to be in charge of your personal choices, take responsibility for your thoughts and actions, and be in control of your life.

The importance of setting intentions appears across a range of contexts, from ancient religions to corporate leadership training programs. Traditional Tibetan meditation begins with a checking-in process to connect deeper aspirations with intentions and motivations. In Stanford University's *Compassion Cultivation Training Program*, every session begins with the practice of *setting your intention*. The idea is to translate this practice to everyday life—to start each day by setting your intention—even developing a specific daily ritual around it. They propose three steps: (1) get settled, relax, and breathe deeply a few times; (2) contemplate what you value deeply and what, deep in your heart, you wish for yourself, others, and the world; and (3) develop a specific set of thoughts as your conscious intention for the day. In this fashion, your intention sets the tone for your day. Then you can check in with yourself at different times of the day and reflect again on your day before you go to bed.

Your intention can be large, reflecting a general strategy for how you want to live your life each day, or it can be small, reflecting a specific goal you are working on. You can rehearse and repeat your intention in your head, or you can write it down if you find doing so helpful. For facilitating compassion broadly in your life, you can start with the Buddhist Four Immeasurables prayer, bearing on the four principles of love, compassion, joy, and equanimity:

> May all sentient beings attain happiness and the causes of happiness.

May all be free from suffering and the causes of suffering.
May they never be separated from the highest bliss, which is devoid of suffering.
May they come to rest in equanimity, which is free of attachment and aversion.

Some people use a prayer like this for their daily intention; others create their own mantra and repeat it every day. Think of this as a guide for living. Reflect on what you value. Here are some other ideas for compassion-driven mantras:

May I be grateful, may I be joyful, may I be kind.
May I be present in the moment.
May I greet this day with a grateful heart.
May I live in this day with loving kindness, tolerance, acceptance, appreciation, understanding, empathy, and compassion.
May I open myself to my feelings and the feelings of others.
May I embrace our common humanity, as we are all one.

You also can frame your intentions in a more specific manner, possibly reflecting a current challenge that you might handle in a more compassionate manner. For example, say you are having difficulties with a coworker. You often find yourself getting mad at the coworker rather than being helpful. You might set your intention by saying something like, "May I respect my coworker as a person who is trying to do a good job, and be helpful whenever I can." If you are trying to eat healthy food and exercise more, you might say, "May I treat my body kindly by eating fresh and healthy food and going for a brisk walk."

Note that your intentions can be different from day to day, or you can use the same one every day. The important thing is that they are meaningful to you and easy for you to remember. To help your actions align with your intentions, keep reminding yourself throughout the day of the value of what you are doing, why it is important, and how you can make it happen.

Do you notice a common theme across the examples we provided? Yes, it is to keep your intentions *positive*. Reflect on and state what you *will do* rather than what you *won't do*. As we mentioned earlier, research has shown that negative emotions and beliefs overpower positive ones. Thinking about a negative emotion can lead you to be more self-critical when you transgress, whereas thinking about a positive emotion will lead you to acknowledge and embrace what you accomplish. Remember, you are enough!

Here is what one of our college students finds most helpful to overcome negative thinking:

> To overcome this negative way of thinking, I perceived these thoughts from a different perspective to try and eliminate this cycle of self-criticism and self-hatred. Instead of telling myself I can't do anything right or I am not good enough, I viewed this in a more realistic and balanced way by reframing it to, 'I may not be good at everything, and that's okay. I will be better next time.' Eliminating this all-or-nothing thinking allows me to acknowledge the fact that nobody is perfect, and that I should not be too harsh on myself.

What inspires you? What energizes you to be more compassionate? Take a few minutes to reflect on how you want to live your life. Do you want to be positive in all your interactions, to always act with gratitude, to be kind to yourself and others? Do you want to love unconditionally, see the goodness around you, and be open to new experiences in the moment? Write your own mantra, then use it over the next few weeks to set your daily intention. Check in with yourself throughout the day. Reflect each night when you go to bed on what you did well, and then congratulate yourself on what went right. You can reset or adjust your intention whenever you need to. Winter always turns into spring and then summer, there is light at the end of the tunnel.

* * * *

Remember, living a life filled with compassion is not an end state or an ultimate destination. It's an ongoing process of decluttering, setting

Figure 4.4 Iguazu Falls, Brazil. Incredible natural beauty.
Source: © Nancy Guerra and Kirk R. Williams

intentions, and reorienting how you perceive and approach the world. It's a transformative journey that you choose to take, day after day, for the rest of your life.

Notes

1 Roster, C. A., Ferrari, J. R., & Junket, M. P. (2016). The dark side of home: Assessing possession "clutter" on subjective well-being. *Journal of Environmental Psychology*, 4632–4641.

2 Saxbe, D. E. & Repetti, R. (2010) No place like home: Home tours correlate with daily patterns of mood and cortisol. *Personality and Social Psychology Bulletin*, *36*, 71–81.

3 Raines, A. et al. (2015). Hoarding and eating pathology: The mediating role of emotion regulation. *Comparative Psychiatry*, *57*, 29–35.

4 Cutting, J. & Armstrong, K. (2016). Facial expression, size and clutter: Inferences from movie structure to emotion judgments and back. *Attention, Perception and Psychophysics*, *78*, 891–901.

5 Vohs, K. D., Redden, J. P., & Rahinel, R. (2013). Physical order produces healthy choices, generosity and conventionality, whereas disorder produces creativity. *Psychological Science*, online.

6 Barnett, P. J. & Kaufman, J. C. (2020). Mind wandering: Framework of a lexicon and musings on creativity. In D. D. Press, D. Cosmelli, & J. C. Kaufman (eds), *Creativity and the wandering mind: Spontaneous and controlled cognition* . Elsevier Academic Press, pp. 3–23.

7 Killingsworth, M. A. & Gilbert, D. T. (2010). A wandering mind is an unhappy mind. *Science*, *330* (6006), 932. 2010. DOI: 10.1126/science.1192439.

8 McKinsey and Company (2017). *How to improve student educational outcomes: New insights from data analytics*. Discussion paper.

9 Robson, D. (2022). *The expectation effect: How mindset can change your world*. Henry Holt and Co.

10 Thomas, W. I. & Thomas, D.S., (1928) *The child in America: Behavior problems and programs*. Knopf.

11 Jinpa, T. (2016). *A Fearless Heart: How the courage to be compassionate can transform our lives*. Avery.

12   Faasse, K. et al. (2019). The influence of side effect information framing on nocebo effects. *Annals of Behavioral Medicine, 53*, 621–629.
13   Hansen, R., (2015). *Hardwiring happiness: The new brain science of contentment, calm and confidence.* Harmony, p. 12.
14   Payne, K., Niemi, L., & Doris, J. (2018). How to think about implicit bias. *Scientific American.*
15   Gladwell, M. (2005) *Blink: The power of thinking without thinking.* Back Bay Books.

References

Barnett, P. J. & Kaufman, J. C. (2020). Mind wandering: Framework of a lexicon and musings on creativity. In D. D. Press, D. Cosmelli, & J. C. Kaufman (eds), *Creativity and the wandering mind: Spontaneous and controlled cognition.* Elsevier Academic Press, pp. 3–23.

Cutting, J. & Armstrong, K. (2016). Facial expression, size and clutter: inferences from movie structure to emotion judgments and back. *Attention, Perception and Psychophysics, 78*, 891–901.

Faasse, K. et al. (2019). The influence of side effect information framing on nocebo effects. *Annals of Behavioral Medicine, 53*, 621–629.

Gladwell, M. (2005) *Blink: The power of thinking without thinking.* Back Bay Books.

Hansen, R. (2015) *Hardwiring happiness: The new brain science of contentment, calm and confidence.* Harmony, p. 12.

Jinpa, T. (2016). *A Fearless Heart: How the courage to be compassionate can transform our lives.* Avery.

Killingsworth, M. A., & Gilbert, D. T. (2010). A wandering mind is an unhappy mind. *Science, 330*(6006), 932. 2010. DOI: 10.1126/science.1192439.

McKinsey and Company (2017). *How to improve student educational outcomes: New insights from data analytics.* Discussion paper.

Payne, K., Niemi, L., & Doris, J. (2018). How to think about implicit bias. *Scientific American.*

Raines, A. et al. (2015). Hoarding and eating pathology: the mediating role of emotion regulation. *Comparative Psychiatry, 57*, 29–35.

Robson, D. (2022). *The expectation effect: How mindset can change your world.* Henry Holt and Co.

Roster, C. A., Ferrari, J. R., & Junket, M. P. (2016). The dark side of home: assessing possession "clutter" on subjective well-being. *Journal of Environmental Psychology,* 4632–4641.

Saxbe, D. E. & Repetti, R. (2010) No place like home: home tours correlate with daily patterns of mood and cortisol. *Personality and Social Psychology Bulletin, 36*, 71–81.

Thomas, W. I. & Thomas, D. S. (1928) *The child in America: Behavior problems and programs.* Knopf.

Vohs, K. D., Redden, J. P., & Rahinel, R. (2013). Physical order produces healthy choices, generosity and conventionality, whereas disorder produces creativity. *Psychological Science,* online.

5

THE LADDER OF COMPASSION

THE SEVEN VIRTUES OF HIGHLY COMPASSIONATE PEOPLE

How do we cultivate compassion? An important first step is to cultivate habits and skills that help us become more compassionate. These habits and skills help us spread good in the world and promote positivity in our lives and the lives of others. In drawing from a vast array of different sources, ranging from philosophy to religion to social science research, we've identified what we call The Seven Virtues of Highly Compassionate People. They are mindfulness, self-awareness, gratitude, perspective taking, empathy, kindness, and altruism. We link these together in a Ladder of Compassion, starting with Step 1 (at the bottom), with virtues that focus on how you understand and experience yourself and others. We then shift to virtues that help you translate compassionate motivation into compassionate action.

Let's go through the virtues one by one. First, we look at the meaning of each virtue and how it connects with compassion. Next, we ask you to rate yourself on a scale of 1–10. This will give you an idea of what you do best or what you might need to work on. (In the spirit of self-compassion, which we discuss in the next chapter, please don't judge yourself harshly if you don't get a high score. Think of this as a constructive suggestion, not a negative self-judgment.) Then, for each virtue, we share suggested tips and techniques for you to practice. If you keep a journal, you may want to write down your answers and comments.

DOI: 10.4324/9781003312437-7

Figure 5.1 The Ladder of Compassion.
Source: © Nancy Guerra and Kirk R. Williams

Step 1: Mindfulness

Perhaps no virtue has received greater attention in recent years than mindfulness. Indeed, mindfulness training programs have found their way into people's lives and into a broad array of organizations, including hospitals, schools, businesses, and prisons, to name a few. Hundreds of mindfulness studies are published each year that attest to its benefits for health and well-being. As we discussed in Chapter 3, people who practice mindfulness are happier, healthier, more focused, less stressed, and more connected to others.[1]

There are many definitions of mindfulness, but the core components are paying attention (on purpose) in the present moment and without judgment. Mindfulness is a non-judgmental, heightened state of awareness of your thoughts, feelings, body sensations, and surrounding environment. It's being fully present without being overly reactive or overwhelmed by what's going on around you. For example, imagine watching your thoughts or emotions float by like clouds in the sky. It's a way of living facilitated through various meditative practices. A common approach, called mindfulness meditation, involves guided contemplation in a quiet space for a time period ranging anywhere from five or 10 minutes to an hour, once or twice per day.

How does mindfulness relate to compassion? Simply stated, it is grounded in an openness to experience, in allowing things to unfold without frustration or anger, in observing the flow of experience.

Mindfulness allows you to pay attention with kindness instead of judgment. For example, if your mind starts to wander, instead of becoming annoyed you can hold this experience in your awareness to better understand it. This helps you cultivate compassion towards yourself, which is an important starting point for living a compassionate life.

In fact, Kristen Neff and Christopher Germer, two leading self-compassion researchers, write in detail about the transformative effects of what they call *mindful self-compassion*. Mindfulness helps you become aware and accepting of experiences that cause you to suffer. As noted in Chapter 8, certain experiences are roadblocks to seeing and responding to suffering, and mindfulness helps you address these roadblocks.

Mindfulness also increases compassion towards others. In a series of experiments observing the benefits of mindfulness meditation, researchers found that people who participated in structured mindfulness meditation were three times more likely than non-participants to help a stranger in need.[2] Why is that? One explanation is that mindfulness promotes acceptance—not only of your own lived experience but also of others' lives. Mindfulness helps you experience subtler emotional states; it can sensitize you to the suffering of others and help you appreciate the interconnectedness of all living beings. Mindfulness allows you to be more empathic, to feel what others feel.[3]

There also are mindfulness meditations that focus exclusively on loving-kindness and compassion. Adapted from traditional Buddhist techniques, these involve meditating on your own well-being and the well-being of others and wishing them happiness, health, and freedom from suffering. In a series of research studies by Barbara Fredrickson and colleagues, practicing loving-kindness meditation was shown to increase positive emotions, strengthen social connections, enhance relationships with others, and increase life satisfaction.[4]

YOUR TURN: Rate your mindfulness skills on a 1–10 scale.

I TRY TO BE PRESENT, IN THE MOMENT, WITHOUT JUDGMENT.

1	2	3	4	5	6	7	8	9	10
Not at all				Somewhat				A lot	

Figure 5.2 Mindfulness Art.
Source: © Nancy Guerra and Kirk R. Williams

Mindfulness Practice

In addition to guided meditations available on various websites, apps, and through various programs, there are many simple mindfulness exercises you can do. It's helpful to set aside some time each day for your mindfulness practice, particularly when you are just getting started. For example, you could schedule a chime to go off every hour on your phone or computer, which invites you into some brief mindfulness practice.

Just as most meditations start with a focus on breathing, you can start your mindfulness journey by simply attending to your breath. You can spend just a minute or two on this, or as long as you like. The breath is a good place to start because it's always with us—we don't have to remember to bring it with us. To begin, sit in a comfortable place, bring attention to your breath as it moves in and out, and feel and follow it as it gently flows. Any time your mind drifts (as it probably will), simply notice your breath without judgment and then gently bring your attention back to it. You might want to set a timer for five or 10 minutes, or whatever time period feels comfortable. As you progress in your practice, try gradually increasing the time you spend sitting still and focusing on your breath.

Another simple strategy of practicing mindfulness is to focus on each of your five senses. Start by sitting in a comfortable chair holding a small piece of fruit in your hand (strawberries work well). Allow yourself about three minutes to experience each of your senses. Sitting in the chair, what sensations do you notice? Do you feel air on your face? What internal sensations do you notice? Now switch to hearing. What do you hear?

Figure 5.3 Mindful moments.
Source: © Nancy Guerra and Kirk R. Williams

Listen to all the sounds around you. Open your eyes and take in what you are seeing. Pay attention to color, depth, height, or anything else that catches your eye. Next, switch to smell. Are there fragrant smells, unpleasant smells, or very few smells? Do you smell the sweet aroma of the fruit in your hand? See if you can breathe slowly through your nose, focusing on your sense of smell. Finally, bite into your fruit very slowly. What flavors are you experiencing? Are they sweet or sour? Does the taste remain for very long? Can you truly appreciate the flavor?

There is one particular practice we like, which begins with taking what you typically consider a mundane task (like folding your laundry). Instead of going through your usual motions on autopilot, take time to experience what you are doing with as many senses as possible. How does the fresh laundry smell? How do the clothes feel in your hands? What does your folded pile look like? Are you aware of any sounds? A benefit of mindfulness practice is that it can take us off autopilot. This allows us to understand our thoughts and sensations for what they are in the moment, rather than falling into habitual and rigid patterns of thought.

There are many ways to increase mindfulness, from short breathing exercises to more focused meditations. Mindfulness can become a way of living, of becoming more aware, in which you take stock of what you feel, see, hear, and so on as part of your daily life. You do not need to sit in a trance-like meditation for hours every day or become a Buddhist monk. Simply focus on what works best for you and what you feel most comfortable with.

Step 2: Self-Awareness

Being self-aware means consciously knowing and understanding yourself, including your needs, habits, emotions, skills, strengths, weaknesses, fears, attitudes, beliefs, purpose, and passion. You must also come to understand what you think, what you do, how you feel and how you act, what inspires you, what ticks you off, and everything that makes you who you are. A vast literature exists in the social and behavioral sciences, particularly psychology, sociology, religion, and philosophy, on the nature of the self. That literature addresses numerous issues about the self, including but certainly not limited to the extent to which we are self-aware, the benefits of self-awareness, how we protect or promote ourselves, and whether our sense of self comes from our own lived experiences or from the input of others. Our concern here is with cultivating self-awareness and linking it to the cultivation of compassion.

Self-awareness is seeing ourselves accurately through our own eyes and knowing our own values, aspirations, passions, thoughts, feelings, behaviors, strengths, and weaknesses. However, understanding how *other* people see us and how they judge these factors is also important. After all, you can be very aware of how you view yourself but not how others see you, or vice versa. Of course, the most self-aware person knows what they want, who they are, and how others see them. Self-awareness also is highly beneficial. Highly aware people express more life satisfaction and happiness, have better relationships with others, and are seen as more effective.

Let us now consider why and how self-awareness might be linked to compassion. First of all, self-awareness is an important component of self-compassion and treating yourself with loving-kindness and acceptance. The more you are aware of and accept your strengths and weaknesses, the less likely you are to be unduly harsh or critical towards yourself. Self-awareness also can help you become a better person. The more self-aware you are, the more open you may be to constructive feedback from others (remember, this is external self-awareness) and building on your strengths and overcoming your weaknesses. This allows you to become a better person, showing compassion not only towards yourself but towards others. The more you can read your own feelings and thoughts, the more capable you become of understanding others.

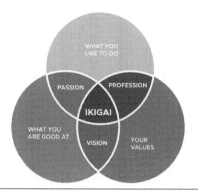

Figure 5.4 Ikigai.
Source: © Nancy Guerra and Kirk R. Williams

Have you heard of the Japanese concept of *ikigai*? The closest translation is your reason for being, or why you get up in the morning. It builds on your internal self-awareness. An easy way to find your ikigai is to make lists of (1) your values, (2) things you like to do, and (3) things you are good at. If you want to translate this into the world of work and engagement, you can add what the world needs and what you can get paid for. Just being aware of and leveraging your strengths, talents, and passion in service of helping others is a great first step.

YOUR TURN: Rate your internal and external self-awareness on a 1–10 scale.
I KNOW WHO I AM, WHAT I WANT, AND MY STRENGTHS AND WEAKNESSES.

1	2	3	4	5	6	7	8	9	10
Not at all				Somewhat				A lot	

I KNOW HOW OTHER PEOPLE SEE ME, WHAT THEY SEE ME AS, AND MY STRENGTHS AND WEAKNESSES.

1	2	3	4	5	6	7	8	9	10
Not at all				Somewhat				A lot	

Self-Awareness Practice

There are many ways to improve both your internal and external self-awareness. You can find entire books dedicated to self-awareness, plus a number of different activities posted online. Here are some suggestions.

Figure 5.5 Who Am I?
Source: © Nancy Guerra and Kirk R. Williams

First, focus on getting to know yourself. A simple technique is to write down your answers to the following question: *Who am I?* Write down whatever comes to mind, with no judgment or censoring. You can use bullet points or full sentences to describe yourself. If you get stuck, think of the different roles you play (e.g., mother, daughter, sister-in-law, employee, etc.) and the characteristics that really make you *who you are* from the inside out.

Another technique is to engage in *self-awareness meditation*. Find a few moments, take a deep breath, and think about who you are and who you want to be. Think about what you are good at, what you want, what you are passionate about, what you love to do, what you want to get better at, what blocks you in your life, and what you need to be the person you want to be. You can also reflect on your ideal self and what kind of person you would like to become.

What is your path forward? Write down what you *want to do* and what you *need to get* in order to get where you want to be. What are your goals, plans, and priorities? It may be helpful to start with the big picture and then break it down into smaller, more tangible, short- and long-term goals.

There also are a number of helpful self-awareness assessments and personality tests you can take. Our undergraduate college students particularly liked the *Clifton Strengths Finder*. Even the short version provides information on your top five strengths, which is a good place to start. You can also take the Big Five or the Myers-Briggs Personality tests, both of which can be found online.

In *The Seven Habits of Highly Effective People,* author Stephen Covey suggests that you write your own eulogy, including what you want people to remember you by, what you want them to say about you at your funeral, and what they will think about you after you are gone. This exercise can help you start thinking about how others see you, your external self-awareness, and your life legacy. How might leading a more compassionate life contribute to the way you are seen by others during your life and remembered by them after your death?

Probably the simplest technique to check your external self-awareness is to talk with your friends, your family, and your colleagues. Ask them how they would describe you, what they think your strengths and weaknesses are, and what they admire about you. This methodology is widely used by businesses—particularly in evaluating leaders and executives—in what is called a *360-comprehensive assessment*. It is called a 360 because it is a full review of how a person's self-view and the views of their peers, supervisors, subordinates, and customers align. It provides a more holistic analysis of a person's strengths and weaknesses, efficiencies, behaviors, and competencies. Finally, it serves to increase one's internal and external self-awareness.

Step 3: Gratitude

Do you spend time reflecting on what is good in your life? Are you thankful for what you have? Do you take time to notice and appreciate all the little things in life, to "stop and smell the roses?" Do you regularly count your blessings? Do you remember to appreciate others often and sincerely? If you do, you are practicing gratitude, which comes from the Latin word "gratus," which means "thankful, pleasing."

Figure 5.6 Daily reminder. We like to post sayings that keep us focused on the good.
Source: © Nancy Guerra and Kirk R. Williams

The importance of gratitude has been acknowledged for centuries throughout many religions and philosophies. As the Greek philosopher Epictetus said, "He is a wise man who does not grieve for the things which he has not, but rejoices for those which he has." Or as Voltaire said, "Appreciation is a wonderful thing. It makes what is excellent in others belong to us as well." More recently, gratitude has been the subject of considerable scientific interest, particularly the effects of gratitude, how it manifests in the brain, and how we can improve or enhance our practice of gratitude.

For example, studies found a connection between gratitude and brain structures associated with social bonding and reward and stress relief, including increases in oxytocin, a chemical that promotes social ties.[5] Other research looked at gratitude from an evolutionary perspective, proposing that gratitude may be essential for survival. It motivates beneficiaries of gratitude to repay their benefactors and lay a foundation for upstream reciprocity or paying it forward.[6] Gratitude is also associated with a host of positive effects, including improved physical and psychological health, increased happiness, lower levels of depression, increased optimism, and better sleep.[7]

Gratitude is good for you, and it is good for others. Gratitude can make you more grounded and better able to help those in need. Gratitude heightens your awareness of how interconnected you are with others and with the world around you, thus offering you a gateway to compassion. When you realize and appreciate the good things in life, it makes you more sensitive to what others may not have, again leading to compassion. And as we will see, there are many easy ways to practice gratitude and lay the groundwork for compassion.

<u>YOUR TURN:</u> Rate your level of gratitude on a 1–10 scale.
I AM GRATEFUL EACH DAY FOR ALL THAT IS POSITIVE AND GOOD IN MY LIFE.

1	2	3	4	5	6	7	8	9	10
Not at all				Somewhat				A lot	

Gratitude Practice

You can find simple gratitude exercises online or in the many books about gratitude. We will now discuss the exercises we try to practice regularly.

An easy and widely used technique for increasing gratitude is to keep a gratitude journal. Start by taking time each week to step outside yourself and reflect on your life. Be aware of the timing that works best for you. This may be every morning or on Friday afternoons at the end of the week. What's important is to pick the timing that fits nicely within your lifestyle. Now, use this time to focus on a few things that you are grateful for in that moment, ranging from the mundane (the warmth of a cup of coffee or tea in your hand) to the magnificent (the sheer beauty of a golden crescent moon). Or you may prefer to focus on one thing you often take for granted (such as being alive) and really, deeply appreciate it.

Another helpful exercise is to express your gratitude directly to someone else. How often do you let people know how much you appreciate something they've done, their friendship, or how important they are to you? Is there someone who comes to mind to whom you owe a debt of gratitude you've never expressed? A teacher, co-worker, colleague, friend, or neighbor? Talk to this person directly or send them an email to detail what they did, how it impacted your life, how important it was to you, and how often you think fondly of it. You can also write a gratitude letter to someone you don't even know whose work or words have made a difference in your life, such as your favorite author or humanitarian.

Ideally, you should personally deliver or send the gratitude message on a special day, such as a birthday or holiday. If you prefer, you can select a nice card and write your words of gratitude on the card. We guarantee that the person who receives your message or card will be uplifted, maybe even on cloud nine, because of your kind words. But did you know that *you* will also experience positive emotions and greater happiness from expressing or sending a gratitude message? Many studies find that expressing gratitude makes you happier. Even if you don't deliver your message, just writing it can bring you joy and improve your well-being.

Another strategy we use is the *three good things* practice, which is a simple technique to help you savor positive events each day. It's pretty self-explanatory—simply spend five to 10 minutes at the end of each day writing about (or just thinking about in detail) three things that went well that day. Allow yourself to remember and appreciate these good things. If you reflect daily on what is good in your life, you will start to see goodness all around you and focus on what is beautiful in your life.

A related technique involves *savoring*, which means intentionally experiencing pleasures that you may often take for granted. For example, someone says something nice to you. You may feel happiness in the moment, but then when you are stuck in traffic 10 minutes later you completely forget about what was said. Rather than ruminate about the traffic, why not replay the kind words that were said to you? Why not keep these kind words central to your awareness so you can bring them back whenever you want? Remember, they are yours forever to savor.

Another way to savor what is pleasurable is to give it up temporarily. That may sound counterintuitive, but taking something you love away and then coming back to it later is a great strategy. Many of us love dessert, whether it be chocolate cake or apple pie. If you abstain from eating dessert for a week and then indulge in your favorite treat, you will ultimately derive greater pleasure from it and feel greater appreciation. (This fact has been confirmed in scientific research.) It's a case in point of absence making the heart grow fonder, and restraint making pleasure that much greater.

Step 4: Perspective Taking

In your daily contacts with people, do you sometimes find yourself wondering what others see or think, literally trying to understand the world through their eyes? That's called *perspective taking*, or in other words, looking beyond your own point of view and taking that of the other. This is different than *empathy*, which is feeling what the other person feels. However, in practice, these terms are often used interchangeably and defined in many different ways. For example, understanding what someone is feeling is often called *affective-perspective taking* by some and *cognitive empathy* by others. To complicate matters further, both perspective taking and empathy have been linked to *mirror neurons* in our brains. These are brain cells that fire when you watch someone do something. They allow you to mimic others, understand their feelings and thoughts, and feel what they feel. In other words, these neurons facilitate both perspective taking and empathy.

We find it helpful, however, to differentiate perspective taking as *knowing* and empathy as *feeling*. Let's focus first on *knowing* what someone else sees and thinks. Imagine you are looking at a suspension bridge over a 200-foot drop. What do you see? Now imagine what a structural engineer would see, what a tourist would see, or what a big-rig truck driver might see. Each person has a somewhat different perspective on what they see because they have different values, needs, and experiences. In short, they have different standpoints on the same bridge.

Our ability to take another's perspective starts in childhood and continues into early adulthood. Young children, usually under age seven or so, have a very hard time figuring out another's point of view. They think everyone views the world just as they do. But as children get older, they are able to take another person's perspective (i.e., a *second person perspective*). During adolescence and early adulthood, this ability develops further so they can step outside of a situation and take a *third-person perspective*. This perspective is similar to how a narrator can exist outside of a story, knowing what is happening in the story without being a part of it.

How is perspective taking connected to compassion? First, perspective taking allows us to be more aware of someone else's suffering, even though we may not experience the same level of suffering. It allows us to understand what the other person needs, which may differ from what we would need in the same situation. Perspective taking also helps us focus on our common humanity, a cornerstone of compassion, rather than in-group favoritism and bias. Indeed, many studies have found that perspective taking leads to reduced bias and prejudice and less in-group favoritism, even reducing what is known as "implicit biases," which lead to more subtle forms of discrimination.

YOUR TURN: Rate your ability to take another person's perspective on a 1–10 scale.

I CAN EASILY PUT MYSELF IN SOMEONE ELSE'S SHOES TO KNOW WHAT THEY SEE OR THINK.

1	2	3	4	5	6	7	8	9	10
Not at all				Somewhat				A lot	

Perspective-Taking Practice

You can get better at taking the perspective of others, but it takes practice. A good place to start is to take a closer look at your own perspective (that is, how you experience life). This requires being self-aware, particularly of the filters you may be looking through. Can you think of any biases that affect how you see certain events? For example, do you believe that a specific person just doesn't understand you, and so in turn you discount the value of what that person says or does? Do you ever dismiss or discount people who have differing political views from yours? Take a few minutes to think about your unique perspective and biases. Try to recall a time you didn't see clearly and then realized you were wrong. What happened?

Practicing mindfulness will also help you get better at perspective taking. Truly understanding someone else's experience requires you to be fully present and give that person your undivided attention. You must listen and observe them carefully, regardless of whether or not you agree with them. Another technique you can use is to write a "day in the life" essay about someone you have a hard time understanding. Pretend that you are that person and you are describing your (their) life.

You can also look at a picture with a group of people in it, preferably one that is relatively ambiguous but with some dramatic features (for example, one person is holding a bouquet of flowers). Now, write a story from each person in the photo's perspective. In other words, imagine that you are each person, then tell "your" story. When you are finished, read over your stories. Were you able to refocus from each character's perspective?

A simple and direct way to practice perspective taking is to role play with another person. This often works well with children. Even young children can role play by using puppets to act out different roles. Friends or couples experiencing relationship conflicts often find it helpful to role play as themselves, switch roles, and then have a discussion about what they learned from the other's perspective. Just be sure to role play a concrete issue or identifiable problem with a clear focus. Understanding what the other person is experiencing can be eye-opening and can help you connect with that person in a more compassionate way.

Step 5: Empathy

Let's turn to our ability to feel what others feel. We are born with empathy—the capacity to share others' emotions. Studies have found that even newborns display more distress when they hear the cry of another newborn. Empathy can be in response to negative or positive emotions, although it usually is stronger in situations involving negative emotions.

Empathy is not the same as sympathy, even though the terms are often confused. Sympathy allows you to feel bad for someone but maintain an emotional distance, such as seeing someone in a deep hole and talking to them from above. Sympathy can be seen as feeling bad or sorry *for* a person. Empathy is feeling *with* the person. In essence, you are climbing down into the hole and sitting next to them.

From an evolutionary perspective, empathy is adaptive. It helps us work together in groups. We have naturally evolved to care for each other and form strong attachment relationships. In recent years in the United States and worldwide, with growing political strife and polarization, "empathy" has been touted as the cure-all. Barack Obama once even noted, "The biggest deficit we have in our society and in the world right now is an empathy deficit." There have been thousands of articles, books, and self-help guides written about empathy and how to increase it. Companies are springing up to provide empathy training for parents, educators, policymakers, business leaders, and health care professionals. For almost every pressing social problem, a lack of empathy is part of the cause, and more empathy is crucial to the cure.

Empathy is often used interchangeably with compassion, although there are important differences. Empathy can facilitate compassion. If you literally feel someone's suffering, you are more likely to be motivated to take action to reduce it. Empathy can direct your attention to where help is needed, but you don't necessarily need to react with empathy to try to reduce someone's suffering. Similarly, you can feel what someone else feels and walk away if you are tired, busy, or distracted. Empathy is a building block of compassion, but it is not enough on its own. To back this up, neuroscience has shown that empathy and compassion even have distinct brain pathways. This is important to keep in mind.

One of the main limits of empathy is that it generally favors the in-group—that is, your friends and family, those close to you, and those who belong to the same groups as you. We discussed this in more detail in Chapter 2. In his recent book, *Against empathy: The Case for Rational Compassion*, psychologist Paul Bloom argues that empathy is biased and that it favors the one over the many and the familiar over the unknown.[8]

Do you find it easier to empathize with people closest to you, who are similar to you or who you see as more appealing?

The real challenge is to extend empathy to those outside our inner circle, including those we don't know. We can even go as far as to consider many of the collective horrors of history as showcasing the limits of empathy, dividing the world into us versus them, increasing allegiance to the in-group at the expense of the out-group, and ignoring our shared humanity.

YOUR TURN: Rate your ability to feel what others feel on a 1–10 scale.
I OFTEN FIND THAT I FEEL WHAT OTHERS ARE FEELING. IF OTHERS ARE HAPPY, I FEEL HAPPY. IF OTHERS ARE SAD, I FEEL SAD.

1	2	3	4	5	6	7	8	9	10
Not at all				Somewhat				A lot	

Empathy Practice

Given the explosion of interest in the importance of empathy, there are numerous exercises and practices you can try. There are even card games and board games designed to promote empathy. We will now share with you some common ideas for increasing empathy in social interactions, with a particular focus on how to extend empathy towards all living beings.

A basic approach to increasing empathy is to pay attention and listen actively (this is labeled as *empathic communication*). This means listening with full attention so you can understand and validate another person's feelings. Don't interrupt; wait until the person is finished talking before responding. And when you do respond, don't plan ahead what you want to say or shift the focus onto yourself. Instead, let your reply be guided by the present moment. Instead of arguing, judging, or trying to counter or deny what someone is feeling (for example, you might normally say, "I don't see why you feel that way; you shouldn't feel that way"), try to acknowledge and restate those feelings (for example, say, "You must feel so hopeless" or "I can see how difficult this has been for you"). Pay attention to a person's body language and facial expressions in addition to their words. In general, *talk less and listen more without critical analysis or judgment.*

An easy technique to increase empathy that can also facilitate compassion is to step outside your comfort zone. Spend time with people you don't know very well, visit new places and meet with locals, attend some-one else's house of worship, follow people from different backgrounds on social media, or talk to people you normally don't interact with and ask them meaningful questions about their lives. We often try to interact with people from different social and political spheres with the explicit goal of finding out what we have in common. There is always something that connects us. Even reading about people from different backgrounds can increase your empathy skills.

In group settings focused on team-building, a simple technique is to put people together who don't know each other and then ask each person to find out three important pieces of information about the other people in their group. You can also join forces with people from other social, economic, and political groups for a common cause.

Some programs that train people in compassion include specific activities to extend empathy to all living beings. In Stanford's *Compassion Cultivation Training*, a major focus is on helping people *recognize* the basic sameness of the self and others, *develop* a deep appreciation of others' well-being, and *expand* their circle of compassion. The program relies heavily on structured meditations. For example, the meditation to expand one's circle of concern begins by meditating on freedom from suffering and wishes for happiness for oneself, then moves on to medi-tating on these issues for a significant and loved other. In the final step, the meditation extends wishes towards a stranger or even someone you find challenging.

Step 6: Kindness

What comes to mind when you think about kindness? How would you define it? Do you consider yourself a kind person? Think about the last time you did something you considered to be kind. What did you do? How did you feel? Now, think about the last time someone acted kindly towards you. What did they do? How did you feel? If you keep a journal, write down your thoughts and feelings.

Although kindness typically is defined as being friendly, generous, and considerate, it is more than just being nice. Being kind involves act-ing out of concern for self and others, both in what you say and what you do. It includes formalities such as saying "please" and "thank you," but it also goes beyond these formalities to include authentic consideration and respect. Kindness involves doing something; it allows you to translate compassionate motivation into compassionate action, including kind thoughts, kind words, or kind deeds. You can be kind to yourself (self-kindness) and to others.

Let's think first about self-kindness, which means generating and acting on feelings of care and comfort toward ourselves. Do you judge yourself harshly or engage in critical self-talk? Do you work until you are exhausted? Or, instead, do you make sure to take care of your needs, accept your weaknesses, and take time to relax and do what you enjoy? Self-kindness is a cornerstone of self-compassion, a topic we will cover in the next chapter. Self-kindness and self-compassion have been linked to lower levels of anxiety and depression and more positive health outcomes.

The importance of kindness towards others has been underscored throughout history, from biblical teachings to poets to ancient philosophers to modern-day writings encouraging us to be kind. In contemporary times, we have organizations and websites devoted entirely to kindness, such as kindness.org, spreadkindness.org, and inspirekindness. com, to name a few.

Perhaps you have practiced random acts of kindness or regularly engage in kind and charitable activities. And by this point in your life, you've likely heard that helping others is good for you. Kindness makes you happier, reduces stress, prevents illness, and can even help you live longer. Being kind has been shown to cause the pleasure and reward centers in

Figure 5.7 Our dog, Ivy. Animals always seem to generate feelings of kindness and compassion.
Source: © Nancy Guerra and Kirk R. Williams

your brain to light up.[9] Kindness is a foundation for compassion; it is an orientation to life that harnesses feelings of warmth and generosity towards self and others. In her recent book, *The Kindness Cure*, author Tara Cousineau defines kindness as *love in action*. She notes, "Kindness is the conduit for the vastness of love's expression."[10]

YOUR TURN: Rate your self-kindness and kindness towards others on a 1–10 scale.

I TRY TO DO THINGS I ENJOY, TAKE CARE OF MYSELF, AND NOT TO BE HARSH OR CRITICAL TOWARDS MYSELF.

1	2	3	4	5	6	7	8	9	10
Not at all				Somewhat				A lot	

I TRY TO BE KIND TOWARDS OTHERS, SPEAK GEN-TLY TO THEM, LISTEN, SAY KIND WORDS, AND DO KIND DEEDS.

1	2	3	4	5	6	7	8	9	10
Not at all				Somewhat				A lot	

Kindness Practice

The best way to cultivate kindness is to practice it. Think of kindness as a muscle that needs exercise to stay strong. There are many examples of strategies that increase kindness towards yourself and others. You can find various websites, articles, and books that have been written on the topic.

We like to start by cultivating feelings of kindness in ourselves. There are several ways to do this. As we mentioned in the section on mindfulness, loving-kindness meditation helps you focus on both your own well-being and the well-being of others. Kindness is an orientation to life that embodies warmth, generosity, and concern for the self and others.

You might also wish to try the *Feeling Connected* strategy. Think about a time you felt a very strong connection to someone else, either through a great success, a great loss, or simply a deep and meaningful conversation. Now describe this experience in writing. The idea behind this exercise is that feeling connected to others fulfills your fundamental need to belong, sensitizing you more to your own needs and the needs of others.

Our colleague at UC Irvine, Paul Piff, has found that simply taking an *awe walk*, that is, marveling in nature, stimulates positive emotions and cultivates feelings of kindness, which translate into kind actions towards others. Perhaps these awesome experiences help you realize that the world is so much bigger than you—that perhaps you are connected to something much larger in the universe. And engaging with the expansiveness of the world makes you less focused on daily hassles and burdens and more focused on the interconnectedness of all living beings.

Let's turn to some practical strategies to translate kind feelings into kind actions. First, think about how you use words to communicate with others. Are your words harsh and critical? Think of a time someone did something you didn't like. What did you say? Was it kind or unkind? What would be the unkind way to express your feelings? What would be the kind way to say the same thing?

And it's more than just words; it's the tone of your voice. Practice speaking in a kind tone of voice compared to a harsh tone of voice. We've learned from our students that there are even kind and unkind ways to communicate via text. Who knew that punctuation marks were unkind? The point is that we have to be extremely careful in both how and what we communicate to others. Words can hurt, but they can also soothe.

Beyond words, there are many ways to act kindly towards yourself and others. A good place to start is by thinking about one thing you can do every day to practice kindness. Each day, write in your journal or on a notepad what you will do that day. In the evening, reflect on what you did, whether it was easy or difficult, and how it made you feel. You can translate this into a bigger strategy that focuses on *random acts of kindness*. Monday through Friday, perform one random act of kindness per day. This can be anything from donating blood to bringing a meal to a sick friend. There literally are hundreds of ideas you can find on the internet. Then write about what you did, what you felt, what surprised you, or what you learned. If you want to do something even bigger, you can start a kindness campaign in your workplace, organization, or community.

Step 7: Altruism

An important component of altruism is focusing on helping others, typically through actions that don't benefit the self, and sometimes even at *a cost* to the self. Altruism is related to kindness in that most all altruistic actions are kind (in other words, friendly, generous, and considerate).

However, not all kind actions are considered altruistic (for example, say-ing "please" is kind but not altruistic).

Altruism often is used synonymously with terms like benevolent, gen-erous, selfless, charitable, and philanthropic. And some definitions of altruism include both concern for the welfare of others and actions to help others. But we find it most useful to consider altruism as *a concrete action to help others regardless of whether it has costs for oneself.* An extremely wealthy person who donates $100,000 to help homeless youth is acting altruistically regardless of net cost to self. We might say that someone with a more limited income who donates $100,000 is displaying even greater altruism. But in both cases, the motivation and end result is to help others in need.

You can think of altruism as the action phase of compassion. As we have discussed, compassion is a sensitivity to suffering coupled with a desire to help. Altruism, in turn, is a behavior that often is triggered by feelings of compassion and translates motivation into action. Keep in mind that you can feel compassion without acting altruistically, and you can act altruistically without always being motivated by compassion. For example, if your neighbor convinces you to donate money to an organiza-tion you've never heard of, you're acting altruistically without necessarily feeling compassion.

Researchers conducted hundreds of studies linking helping behaviors to a person's health and well-being. Studies ranged from those on the conditions under which people are more likely to help others to the ben-eficial effects of altruistic behaviors, including volunteering and donating to charities. And even though altruism, by definition, is designed to help others without a specific benefit to the self, there is consistent evidence that altruistic people are happier, healthier, and live longer.[11] Altruism is written in our DNA; from an evolutionary perspective, it is easy to see how helping others promotes the survival of our species. Neuroscience research shows that altruism activates the pleasure centers in our brains. We are wired to behave altruistically![12]

In considering the important role that altruism plays in translating compassionate motivation into compassion action to reduce suffering, it is important to think about how we can encourage and harness our altru-istic tendencies and try to do the "most good" that we can. Here is where the concept of *Effective Altruism (EA)* comes into play. This is a growing social movement that emphasizes using evidence and reasoning to find ways to benefit others as much as possible. It started with organizations like *Giving What We Can, Givewell,* and *80,000 Hours,* and it rests on the idea that we should begin by prioritizing problems that are great in scale, neglected, and solvable.

What we do next depends on what we are best at and where we can be most helpful. One thing we can do is choose a job or career that helps solve these high-priority problems. Alternatively, we can also work in a highly-paid field and donate money to effective charitable organizations that work to solve these problems. The central issue is how to use your time and money to reduce as much suffering as possible, with actions that are motivated by compassion but driven by reason. Paul Bloom calls this *rational compassion*; that is, combining a desire to make the world a better place with a rational assessment of how best to do so.

YOUR TURN: Rate your overall orientation to help others and your commitment to Effective Altruism on a 1–10 scale.

I TRY TO HELP OTHERS OFTEN, EVEN IF THERE ARE PERSONAL COSTS TO ME.

1	2	3	4	5	6	7	8	9	10
Not at all				Somewhat				A lot	

I CONSIDER MYSELF TO BE AN EFFECTIVE ALTRUIST, ALWAYS TRYING TO DO THE MOST GOOD I CAN DO.

1	2	3	4	5	6	7	8	9	10
Not at all				Somewhat				A lot	

Altruism Practice

There are small ways and big ways to increase your helping and altruistic actions. Let's start with some simple suggestions.

A good first step is to write down or note in your journal at the end of each week all the large and small ways you helped others. This can include those you helped, what you did, what benefits your actions had for others, or what the costs were to you. You may be surprised how some of the smallest things you did—like a few kind words when someone was sad—can be extremely meaningful and helpful to others. After you've done this for a few weeks, try to visualize what you might do to be even more helpful. Start your day by closing your eyes and visualizing yourself helping others in different ways.

Another strategy is to perform one helpful deed a day until it becomes part of your daily routine. Help out with chores at home, or ask a colleague how you can help. We've found that when our children or friends talk with us about something they are struggling with, instead of saying "Oh don't worry, it will work out," it's much more effective to say, "How can I help?"

It's always important to leverage your strengths and passions to help others. What are you best at? What can you do that other people struggle with? What resources do you have that you are comfortable sharing with or giving to others? What do you care most about? This is where self-awareness comes in. You need to know yourself, what motivates you, what energizes you, what you are good at, and what is within your comfort zone.

On a larger scale, think about how you might become an effective altruist. What would be the next step for you? Just looking at different websites that provide guidance, details, and choices for giving is a good place to start. (We mentioned a few such websites earlier in this chapter.) You can also sign up for newsletters from agencies such as *effectivealtruism.org* to learn more about the movement. There are events and virtual communities you can join. You can pledge a percent of your income to effective charities. The important point is to use both your heart and your head to maximize the impact of your altruistic actions.

* * * *

We've now gone through each of the seven virtues linked to compassion. We've asked you to rate yourself on each and suggested several tips and techniques to help you translate these virtues into everyday habits. Remember, the idea is not to judge yourself; it's to learn and make changes in your life. Leverage what you are good at, and work on what you need to improve.

Although we've described the virtues one by one, they are interconnected. For example, as you become more empathic, you are likely also to become kinder and more altruistic. We link these virtues together sequentially in a Ladder of Compassion primarily to underscore the importance of starting with *yourself*. Begin by knowing yourself and practicing mindfulness and gratitude. In doing so, you can build a foundation for connecting more deeply with others. We also want you to start with a keen awareness of your thoughts and feelings, then use that awareness as a foundation for translating compassionate motivation into compassionate actions.

We realize, however, that we each have different life circumstances. Some of us may live in conditions of extreme adversity, whereas others may live a life of privilege. You might ask yourself whether compassion, then, is a luxury for the privileged. Why would anyone cultivate a life of compassion if they feel that their world shows no compassion for them or those like them? Wouldn't it be more natural to respond with resentment, hostility, anger, and perhaps even retaliation? No, it wouldn't, because feeling unhappy or angry in the face of adversity does nothing to eliminate it. In fact, it will likely only aggravate your own anxiety and despair.

Instead, we can rely on the seven virtues to help us understand and overcome difficult circumstances. Our self-awareness can help us identify talents or strengths, which we can harness to improve our situation. Mindfulness and gratitude can orient us towards things that are satisfying in our lives. Even under the direst circumstances, we can find gratitude in some aspect of our lives. In fact, we are reminded of some of our UCI undergraduates, who once traveled to a small village in Ghana for a service-learning experience. After two days without water in the village, the water truck arrived. The students recounted how the young children jumped for joy, making them realize how privileged they were just to have running water back at home. Our students in Peru, who had come from very modest backgrounds themselves, were so taken by the poverty they

Figure 5.8 Global Service Scholars becoming part of life in Peru.
Source: © Nancy Guerra and Kirk R. Williams

witnessed in Peru that they started a GoFundMe page to raise money for pencils and paper for students in the school where they were working.

Through kindness and altruism towards ourselves and others, we can be part of alleviating global suffering. Together, we can work to make the world a better place. As Mahatma Gandhi said, "Be the change you wish to see in the world."

Notes

1   Halliwell, E. (2015). *Mindfulness made easy: Learn how to be present and kind to yourself and others*. UK: Hay House.
2   Lim, D., Condon, P., & DeSteno, D. (2015). Mindfulness and Compassion: An examination of mechanism and scalability. *PLOS ONE, 10* (2): e0118221.
3   Shapiro, S. L., Schwartz, G. E., & Bonner, G. (1998). Effects of mindfulness-based stress reduction on medical and premedical students. *Journal of Behavioral Medicine, 21* (6), 581–599.
4   Fredrickson, B. L., Cohn, M. A., Coffey, K. A., Pek, J., & Finkel, S. M. (2008). Open hearts build lives: positive emotions, induced through loving-kindness meditation, build consequential personal resources. *Journal of Personality and Social Psychology, 95* (5), 1045.
5   Algoe, S. & Way, B. (2014). Evidence for a role of the oxytocin system, indexed by genetic variation in CD38, in the social bonding effects of expressed gratitude. *Social Cognitive and Affective Neuroscience, 9* (12), 1855–1861.
6   McCullough, M., Kimeldorf, M., & Cohen, A. (2008). An adaptation for altruism: The social causes, social effects and social evolution of gratitude. *Current Directions in Psychological Science, 17* (4), 281–285.
7   Sansone, R. & Sansone, L. (2010). Gratitude and well-being: The benefits of appreci-ation. *Psychiatry*, Nov, 7 (11) 18–22.
8   Bloom, P. (2016). *Against empathy: The case for rational compassion.* HarperCollins.
9   Mayo Clinic (2020). *The art of kindness.* https://www.mayoclinichealthsystem.org/hometown-health/speaking-of-health/the-art-of-kindness
10   Cousineau, T. (2018). *The kindness cure: How the science of compassion can heal your heart and your world.* Oakland, CA: New Harbinger Publications.
11   Brown, W. M., Considine, N. S., & Magai, C. (2005). Altruism relates to health in an ethnically diverse sample of older adults. *J Gerontol B Psychol Sci Soc Sci., 60* (3), 143–152. doi: 10.1093/geronb/60.3. p143. PMID: 15860784.
12   Filkowski, M. M., Cochran, R. N., & Haas, B. W. (2016). Altruistic behavior: Mapping responses in the brain. *Neuroscience and Neuroeconomics, 5*, 65–75. https://doi.org/10.2147/NAN.S87718.

References

Algoe, S. & Way, B. (2014). Evidence for a role of the oxytocin system, indexed by genetic variation in CD38, in the social bonding effects of expressed gratitude. *Social Cognitive and Affective Neuroscience*, 9(12), 1855–1861.
Bloom, P. (2016). *Against empathy: The case for rational compassion.* HarperCollins.
Brown, W. M., Considine, N. S., & Magai, C. (2005). Altruism relates to health in an ethnically diverse sample of older adults. *J Gerontol B Psychol Sci Soc Sci., 60*(3), 143–152. doi: 10.1093/geronb/60.3. p143. PMID: 15860784.

Cousineau, T. (2018). *The kindness cure: How the science of compassion can heal your heart and your world*. Oakland, CA: New Harbinger Publications.

Filkowski, M. M., Cochran, R. N., & Haas, B. W. (2016). Altruistic behavior: Mapping responses in the brain. *Neuroscience and Neuroeconomics*, 5, 65–75. https://doi. org/10.2147/NAN.S87718.

Fredrickson, B. L., Cohn, M. A., Coffey, K. A., Pek, J., & Finkel, S. M. (2008). Open hearts build lives: Positive emotions, induced through loving-kindness meditation, build consequential personal resources. *Journal of Personality and Social Psychology*, 95(5), 1045.

Halliwell, E. (2015*). Mindfulness made easy: Learn how to be present and kind to yourself and others*. UK: Hay House.

Lim, D., Condon, P., & DeSteno, D. (2015). Mindfulness and compassion: An examination of mechanism and scalability. *PLOS ONE*, 10(2), e0118221.

Mayo Clinic (2020). *The art of kindness*. https://www.mayoclinichealthsystem.org/hometown-health/speaking-of-health/the-art-of-kindness

McCullough, M., Kimeldorf, M., & Cohen, A. (2008). An adaptation for altruism: The social causes, social effects and social evolution of gratitude. *Current Directions in Psychological Science*, 17(4), 281–285.

Sansone, R. & Sansone, L. (2010). Gratitude and well-being: The benefits of appreciation. *Psychiatry*, Nov, 7(11), 18–22.

Shapiro, S. L., Schwartz, G. E., & Bonner, G. (1998). Effects of mindfulness-based stress reduction on medical and premedical students. *Journal of Behavioral Medicine*, 21(6), 581–599.

6

PRACTICING SELF-COMPASSION

We've talked quite a bit about acting with compassion towards others, whether that means friends, family, or complete strangers. Compassion embraces what unites us, our common humanity. You may not have thought too much about this, but common humanity also includes YOU! Yes, you are part of the human condition we all share, however imperfect it may be. And you struggle in your own way to navigate the human condition with joy and happiness rather than sadness and sorrow.

This means that your compassionate feelings and actions need to include how you treat yourself. We call this *self-compassion*. It is compassion directed inward instead of outward. Think about this for a moment. Imagine the last time you made a mistake or did something foolish. Go over what happened in your mind. Now, reflect on how you experienced the moment. What did you tell yourself? Did you say, "That's okay, you're just human. You'll do better next time." Or were you critical of yourself? Which was it?

Now, think about what you would have said to a friend who did the same thing. If you're like most people, you're likely much kinder to your friend than to yourself. You probably would have told your friend, "Don't worry, we all make mistakes," or tried to cheer them up some other way.

DOI: 10.4324/9781003312437-8

Figure 6.1 Kirk taking a moment of self-reflection on a Southern California beach.
Source: © Nancy Guerra and Kirk R. Williams

You probably didn't say anything critical or discouraging. Most of us are kinder to our friends than we are to ourselves. As one of our undergraduate students once stated, "If I talked to my friends the way I talk to myself, I wouldn't have any friends."

Where does this negative self-talk come from? Why would you treat yourself this way? Doesn't it make more sense to be kind to yourself, to give yourself space to make mistakes and learn from them? And can you really extend care and compassion to others if you don't care for and love yourself? These are difficult and important questions that we will try to answer in this chapter. We'll also try to give you some concrete tips on how to become more self-compassionate, and we'll touch on why doing so is important.

How Self-Compassionate Are You?

Kristin Neff, a leading figure in the field of self-compassion, talks about three central components of self-compassion: *self-kindness vs. self-judgment*; *common humanity vs. isolation*; and *mindfulness vs. over-identification*. These components work together to create a self-compassionate frame of mind, a way of being that allows us to be touched by our own suffering and to respond with kindness. Take a moment to complete the Self-Compassion Scale below, then calculate your score. This scale was created and validated by Kristin Neff, and she generously makes it available for free on her website (https://self-compassion.org/).

Self-Compassion Scale

1. When I fail at something important to me, I become consumed by feelings of inadequacy.

   Almost Always = 1   2   3   4   5 = Almost Never

2. I try to be understanding and patient towards those aspects of my personality I don't like.

   Almost Never = 1   2   3   4   5 = Almost Always

3. When something painful happens, I try to take a balanced view of the situation.

   Almost Never = 1   2   3   4   5 = Almost Always

4. When I'm feeling down, I tend to feel like most other people are probably happier than I am.

   Almost Always = 1   2   3   4   5 = Almost Never

5. I try to see my failings as part of the human condition.

   Almost Never = 1   2   3   4   5 = Almost Always

6. When I'm going through a very hard time, I give myself the caring and tenderness I need.

   Almost Never = 1   2   3   4   5 = Almost Always

7. When something upsets me, I try to keep my emotions in balance.

   Almost Never = 1   2   3   4   5 = Almost Always

8. When I fail at something that's important to me, I tend to feel alone in my failure.

   Almost Always = 1   2   3   4   5 = Almost Never

9. When I'm feeling down, I tend to obsess and fixate on everything that's wrong.

   Almost Always = 1   2   3   4   5 = Almost Never

10. When I feel inadequate in some way, I try to remind myself that feelings of inadequacy are shared by most people.

    Almost Never = 1   2   3   4   5 = Almost Always

11. I'm disapproving and judgmental about my own flaws and inadequacies.

    Almost Always = 1   2   3   4   5 = Almost Never

12. I'm intolerant and impatient towards those aspects of my personality I don't like.

    Almost Always = 1   2   3   4   5 = Almost Never

Scoring. Now, add your scores to create a total score. With 12 items, your total score should range from 12 to 60. Take your total score and divide it by 12. This gives you an average total score that should range between 1 and 5. If you scored between 1 and 2.49, you would be classified as **low** in self-compassion. If you scored between 2.5 and 3.5, you would be **moderate** in self-compassion. And if you scored between 3.51 and 5, your level of self-compassion is considered **high**. Keep in mind, this still is just a ballpark gauge for assessing your level of self-compassion, not a definitive determination chipped in stone.

So, where did you land on this classification? If you're in the high category, congratulations! You treat yourself with loving-kindness. If you're in the low or moderate category, stay tuned. We will talk about some of the reasons we are all so hard on ourselves, how to alleviate and even prevent your own suffering, and how to apply some of the seven virtues of highly compassionate people to the practice of self-compassion.

We have talked about compassion not only as a means to alleviate suffering but as a way to prevent suffering from happening in the first place. We also talked about how compassion compels us to do good in the world and promote peace, harmony, happiness, and joy. When we talk about self-compassion, we are talking about both alleviating our suffering and healing ourselves with kindness. We also are talking about how to navigate and understand our world so that we may prevent our own suffering and promote our own health and well-being.

Self-Compassion: The Wabi Sabi Way

Have you ever heard of the Wabi Sabi approach to living? It is an approach based on an ancient Japanese philosophy that includes some basic principles for living. Wabi Sabi embraces the beauty in imperfection and encourages us to accept the natural cycle of life. Stated simply, *nothing is perfect, nothing is finished, and nothing lasts.* These principles are quite relevant to compassion towards all living things, but they are particularly relevant when we think about self-compassion. Just as everything in life is imperfect, incomplete, and impermanent, so too are humans. Approaching life with this thought in mind encourages us to accept what is, stay in the moment, and be grateful for the simple things in life. It gives us tools to respond to suffering in our own life and prevent the suffering we bring upon ourselves.

What Causes Us to Suffer?

Suffering is often unavoidable. For example, a death in the family, a serious illness, or a natural disaster are cases of suffering we can't avoid. There is considerable agreement across philosophical, educational, religious, and spiritual traditions that suffering is an inevitable part of life. But there also is agreement that humans *cause* a lot of suffering—not only to others but to ourselves. A first step towards self-compassion is to be aware of the ways we inflict suffering on ourselves. Take a moment to think about different ways you actually create your own suffering. A Wabi Sabi framework reminds us that change is inevitable and that nothing is perfect; yet, our resistance to change, our quest for perfection, and our disconnection from nature and all forms of life contribute greatly to our suffering.

Resistance to Change

A basic principle of Wabi Sabi living is the fundamental acceptance of the impermanence of nature. This principle refers to the undeniable fact that all things in nature are constantly changing, with the most obvious example being ourselves. We go through sequential phases of life between birth to death. Psychologists refer to this as the life course. Clearly, each phase of the life course is associated with all kinds of changes in our bodies and how we think, feel, and act. Wherever you are in this life course, think about how different you are now compared to where you've been. How much change do you see? Do you realistically think that you will

Figure 6.2 The life course.
Source: © Nancy Guerra and Kirk R. Williams

no longer change in any way as you continue on your life journey? The point is that we are not born into this world as complete beings. We go through numerous transitions that dynamically construct and reconstruct who we are as we age.

This unfolding process is not unique to humans. Virtually all of nature has its cycle of life. A plant begins with the germination of seeds to growing roots, sprouting shoots, and flowering adult plants, which produce more seeds and thus start the process over again. Even Earth is undergoing constant change. Geologists who study its history offer deep and rich knowledge of this change. They tell us that the size, shape, and geographic location of what we now know as continents and oceans have changed throughout time. When geologists talk about time, they are not referring to days, weeks, months, and years. They use geologic time, which is divided into eons, eras, periods, and epochs that consist of segments measured in millions—even billions—of years. Keep in mind that our planet is estimated to be 4.6 billion years old. So, as you take a stroll to enjoy the great outdoors, know that the ground beneath you has been changing for billions of years, although at an imperceptible pace.

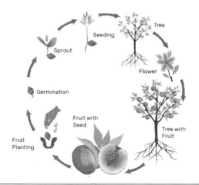

Figure 6.3 The life cycle of a flowering plant.
Source: © Nancy Guerra and Kirk R. Williams

And yet, we often fight against and resist change, and we suffer as a consequence. For example, take the anti-aging industry, a multi-billion-dollar enterprise fed by our desperate desire to stay young. It's staggering to realize that in a single year alone, the global anti-aging market consists of about 62.6 billion U.S. dollars.[1] Instead of embracing aging as a natural part of life, we often turn it into something to avoid or deny at all costs, and we suffer as a consequence.

The Quest for Perfection

If everything is changing and nothing can ever be complete, what does that say about perfection? The Wabi Sabi answer is that perfection is an unachievable goal. Why is it, then, that so many people across so many situations seem to be obsessed with perfection? We live in a world of imperfection, yet we relentlessly pursue perfection. This presents a major source of suffering for us. It's a fanciful pursuit that can only lead to frustration, disappointment, self-doubt, and self-criticism. The quest for perfection is a major source of our own suffering.

Our day-to-day living is replete with high energy expectations. Pressures to achieve and live a life of perfection are as pervasive as the air we breathe. Think about it. We have pressures to achieve favor from family and friends, to achieve at school, to achieve at work, to achieve status in the eyes of others, to achieve a high salary, to achieve promotions, to be attractive, and on and on. This pressure is amplified through social media, where social comparison is the primary currency, and anyone can photoshop themself into perfection.

Indeed, some people become so obsessed with having the perfect body or facial appearance that they create unrealistic images of themselves in their heads or through other avenues. Do you know people who create more attractive pictures of themselves using some form of image editing software—perhaps even Deepfakes—to post pictures on social media? Such activity testifies to our obsession with appearance and how good we look compared to others.

Let's face it. We live in an intensely competitive society, which ultimately leads to invidious comparisons between ourselves and others. We compare ourselves to others in terms of our appearances, but such comparisons are not limited to that issue. We compare ourselves to others in terms of how well we do at school, at work, financially, or in our general quality of life. Interpersonal comparisons based on competition too often result in polarization and, unfortunately, divisiveness and even violence. They surely don't facilitate unity, harmony, and collaborative well-being. Further, such comparisons too often result in a downward spiral of negative feelings of low self-worth, low self-confidence, and self-doubt. Suffice it to say that these conditions of day-to-day living interfere with the promotion of self-compassion. (We discuss this issue further in Chapter 8 on *Barriers to Compassion.*) In her book, *Wabi Sabi: Japanese wisdom for a perfectly imperfect life*, Beth Kempton talks about this. She notes how so many of us have become increasingly motivated by money, prestige, appearance, and the endless accumulation of stuff, leading us to be overworked, overstretched, and overwhelmed with the quest for what we have come to believe is the perfect life.[2]

Does this resonate with you? Do you endlessly pursue perfection within the frenetic context of your life? Do you hear the voices of your peers, parents, and culture (via social media) encouraging you to be perfect—to acquire (at virtually any cost) the valued possessions of our time and/or live up to expectations of what kind of person you should be? Do you hear those voices, including your own, chastising you for not doing so perfectly?

For some people, the quest for perfection is exacerbated by beliefs about success held by different cultural groups or families. For example, we've heard from many of our students and friends that the need to excel, to be perfect, is drilled into them from a very young age. Failure to achieve perfection is met with criticism, shame, or punishment. One student noted that when he received 99/100 on a test, instead of commending him for a job well done, his father asked him where the other point was. This pressure to achieve creates its own type of suffering.

Have you heard of the Japanese art of *Kintsugi*? Consistent with the Wabi Sabi philosophy that nothing is perfect, Kintsugi shows us how to repair a broken object so it can be useful. In fact, rather than trying to hide the cracks or imperfections, they are embraced. Indeed, precious metals (gold, silver) are used to highlight imperfections. The idea is that we must accept imperfection and break free from the stress that perfectionism causes, keeping in mind that past failures should not derail us but instead motivate us to continue forward.

Figure 6.4 Kintsugi—the cracks are highlighted in gold.
Source: © Nancy Guerra and Kirk R. Williams

Disconnecting from Nature

One of the cornerstones of self-compassion is an awareness of our common humanity. When something challenging or upsetting happens to us, it is important to keep in mind that *everyone* faces similar issues. We all experience disappointment, failure, pain, and isolation. Yet, we tend to think we are unique, that this only happens to us, that everyone else is leading a charmed life full of pleasure and happiness. We cut ourselves off from our connections with others, from our connection with the bigger picture. Kristen Neff includes common humanity as one of her key components of self-compassion.

Given the pressures of modern life and the increasingly urban environment we live in, we have also become increasingly disconnected from nature. Yet nature plays a critical role in reinforcing our connection to life and everything living. This deep connection with nature is a fundamental premise of *biophilia*, which literally means the love of life and everything living.

This concept was originally coined by the German psychologist Eric Fromm in his book *The heart of man: Its genesis for good and evil*. He used the concept to describe a psychological orientation or attraction to all that is alive and vital. Edward O. Wilson further developed the concept of *biophilia* in his book on the subject. He used the term in reference to an evolutionary adaptation—an innate focus on and desire to affiliate with life and life-like forms. The key point here is that our attraction to and fascination with nature and all living creatures is inscribed on our biological birth certificate. It allows us to realize we are part of something bigger than ourselves. As Dr. Qing Li discusses in his book, *Forest bathing: How trees can help you find health and happiness*, connecting to nature is the best way to experience something larger than ourselves, to take our breath away and at the same time to breathe new life into us.[3]

Think about a walk you take in the forest. When done mindfully, meaning being fully in the present moment and opening ourselves to our surroundings, we can enliven our senses and at least temporarily transcend ourselves and the trials and tribulations of everyday living.

Psychologists use the term *awe* to describe these experiences. Experiences of awe are vast, larger than life, and transcend our current understanding of the world, meaning they are beyond what words can describe in the moment. Such experiences allow us to get outside ourselves and merge with the indescribable beauty and mystery of the immediate natural environment, our planet, and the mystery of the universe. Moments of awe reinforce our connections with all things living, bringing our common humanity front and center.

What Keeps Us from Attending to Our Own Suffering?

Remember two key components of how we defined compassion. It involves (1) a concern for suffering and (2) a desire to prevent or alleviate that suffering. We further elaborated on concern for suffering as involving attentiveness, meaning how we orient ourselves to a heightened awareness of suffering. We also have an emotional response to suffering;

Figure 6.5 Ushuaia, Patagonia, Argentina. One of the most beautiful places on Earth.
Source: © Nancy Guerra and Kirk R. Williams

we either turn away from it, or find ourselves drawn to do something based on how we interpret it.

Curiously, although it's hard not to be aware of our own suffering, we often find it easier to attend to and react emotionally to the suffering of others. We may feel unhappy or sad for whatever reason and yet push these feelings away as part of our busy lives. If a friend tells us about a stressful situation, we listen attentively. But we often listen less to our own voices and emotions, sometimes even drowning our sorrows in drugs, alcohol, food, or some other diversion.

Is Self-Compassion Selfish?

One reason we attend less to ourselves than others is the misguided belief that self-compassion is selfish. Many people we've talked to about compassion tell us how difficult it is to find a balance between taking care of themselves and taking care of others. They think nothing of going out of their way to help a friend or family member, but they often attend so much to others that they don't take time for themselves. Not only are they harder on themselves than anyone else in the face of their stresses and struggles, they don't allow any time for rest, rejuvenation, self-care, and self-compassion.

When we ask people why they put themselves last, the most common answer we hear is, "It feels selfish to focus too much on myself." Sometimes this feeling comes from cultural norms about putting others first, whether it be a collectivistic orientation to social exchange or beliefs about the centrality of family and putting family first. Other times it comes from the belief that time spent on oneself translates to neglecting those you care about—in other words, being selfish.

But what does it really mean to be selfish? Isn't selfishness putting yourself first at all costs and concentrating solely on your own pleasure or advantage, regardless of the impact it has on others? A selfish person is someone who gets to the table first and eats all the food, without considering the hungry people who are on their way. A self-compassionate person takes time to be kind and nurturing to themself, to meet their own emotional needs, so they are better able to take care of others. Stated simply, we don't need to treat ourselves badly in order to be kind and caring towards others. In fact, the opposite is true: The kinder we are to ourselves, the kinder we can be to others.

In fact, many research studies have observed whether (1) self-criticism interferes with compassion towards others and (2) whether people who practice self-compassion are better able to get along with, care for, and support others. Although the research about whether self-compassion actually is necessary to practice compassion towards others is unclear, it seems a bit like common sense to assume this to be true. Isn't it true that we can only love and understand others if we love and understand ourselves?

Studies certainly have shown that people who practice self-compassion are better able to be compassionate towards others and to sustain that compassion over time. Self-compassion tends to be associated with greater satisfaction in relationships because self-compassionate people have more emotional resources to give their partners. In one study by Kristin Neff and Natasha Beretvas, higher levels of self-compassion were associated with higher levels of positive relationship behaviors as rated by their partners.[4] In another study that observed helping professionals, those who practice self-compassion were less likely to experience caregiver burnout and more likely to feel happier and grateful for being able to make a difference in the world.[5]

Is Self-Criticism Necessary to Excel?

Another common reason why people are reluctant to practice self-compassion is the belief that not performing their best or accepting failure interferes with success. Why accept a "B" when "A" stands for excellent and "B" just stands for good? Kristin Neff notes that one of the biggest blocks to self-compassion is the belief that it undermines motivation, that it will allow us to stop short of our goals.[6]

Think about the last time you performed poorly at a task. Most likely, your first reaction was simply an awareness that you didn't do well. You can't possibly motivate yourself to do better if you don't realize that you did poorly. But what comes *next* is key. If you beat yourself up with personal attacks on your ability, and you see this ability as a fixed trait that can't change, then you are far more likely to derail your motivation. On the other hand, if you realize that, like everyone else, sometimes you simply do better or worse than others, and you try to learn from your experience and do better next time, you will feel motivated to push forward. You don't need to beat yourself up for not trying hard enough. You simply need to realize that your failure is an opportunity for learning, and that you can get better at almost anything you set your mind to.

This strategy is captured in a well-known model of achievement motivation developed by a leading contemporary psychologist, Carol Dweck. Known as *Mindset*, the idea is that success comes from a *growth mindset*. This way of thinking emphasizes that ability is not fixed or carved in stone, but that through effort and experience we can cultivate the qualities we strive to achieve. Setbacks do not lead to self-criticism and giving up; rather, they motivate us to learn and do better.[7] And research has shown that more self-compassionate people have less fear of failure, and when confronted with failure they are more likely to try again.[8] (Just be sure not to let your mindset slip into constantly striving for perfection; just do what you do best and be grateful for what you've accomplished.)

Practicing Self-Compassion: The Seven Virtues

In Chapter 5, we discussed the seven virtues of compassionate people: mindfulness, self-awareness, gratitude, perspective taking, empathy, kindness, and altruism. We proposed that each of these virtues is like a rung on a ladder. So, cultivating each is tantamount to climbing the ladder to achieve compassion in your life. How does this apply to self-compassion? Four rungs of this ladder are particularly relevant in this case—mindfulness, self-awareness, gratitude, and kindness. These are critical levers for self-compassion that work in harmony with each other.

Let's start with mindfulness, which involves a nonjudgmental awareness of the present moment. It allows us to be still, with a heightened sensitivity to our being in the here and now. Practicing mindfulness enhances connections to our thoughts, feelings, physical sensations, and the sights and sounds surrounding us. This state of being is the fertile ground for becoming more attentive to our own suffering and the sources of that suffering. Meditation and deep breathing help us become more mindful. A breathing technique that we find useful is to imagine you are breathing in energy and warmth with each deep breath you take, then exhale any stress and negativity you have inside. Do this for at least three minutes to start, then progress to longer times.

Mindfulness also sets the stage for self-awareness. Moments of nonjudgmental stillness and serenity allow us to see ourselves accurately.

We can be in touch with our thoughts, feelings, and circumstances of our being. It's as if we step outside ourselves as independent observers and look within. Such self-observation reveals our suffering. We can see all its manifestations. That vision allows us to dive deep into what lies beneath our suffering and pinpoint where it's coming from. In that space, we may hear the voices of others, including our own, crying out for perfection in who we are, including our bodies, identities, relationships, and personal accomplishments. That deep dive puts us in a position to respond to the voices by saying, "No, I accept myself for who I am, with all my imperfections, just like everyone else."

This self-awareness pushes you to practice acceptance of who you are without judgment. Since you, like everything in life, are impermanent and thus incomplete, pursuing perfection will only send you down an endless rabbit hole of self-doubt and self-criticism, which leads to negative self-talk. Now, are we telling you to give up and not focus on doing well in life? The answer is an emphatic NO! We just want you to do the best you can under your current circumstances. Accept and appreciate that you have done your best and be content with who you are, what you accomplish, and where you're headed. Slow down, take a deep breath, and silence the voices—including your own—that keep calling for you to be someone you're not.

Achieving self-awareness leads us to the next rung on the ladder: gratitude. We too often obsess over who we are not and what we don't have. That obsession is obviously intricately entwined with our quixotic pursuit of perfection, which, as noted, often results in self-loathing and feelings of failure and worthlessness. With self-awareness, we can accept *and* be grateful for who we truly are and what we actually have. Learning to acknowledge, accept, and appreciate the beauty within and around us will allow gratitude to blossom within us. Gratefully attending to such beauty brings sunshine into an otherwise cloudy day. Complete the first sentence in the box, then say the last sentence out loud.

I am just so very GRATEFUL during this moment, to have ....
I take so much for granted when there is so much to be GRATE-
FUL for.

With self-awareness of our suffering and its sources, coupled with gratitude for who we are with all our imperfections, we are now ready to take action. How shall we treat ourselves? We may answer this question by stepping on the next rung of the ladder toward self-compassion. Instead of all the derisive self-talk, sulking, and beating ourselves up, cultivate gratitude in our lives. It encourages us to be forgiving of our shortcomings and gently sooth ourselves with the same loving-kindness we would extend to a suffering friend, family member, or wounded animal, particularly a cherished pet. A plan of action based on loving-kindness will surely enhance our well-being more than negative self-talk and self-flagellation.

The Benefits of Self-Compassion

Let's turn briefly to a discussion of the known benefits of self-compassion. We've mentioned some of the benefits of having compassion for others. Contrary to the idea that self-compassion makes us focus too much on ourselves at the expense of others, self-compassion actually makes us better at tending to and caring for others. Self-compassion is an important tool for living a compassionate life.

What are some of the benefits FOR YOU of practicing self-compassion? Many research studies have been conducted on this topic, and they found a host of short-term and long-term benefits. For example, self-compassion is associated with better mental health outcomes across diverse populations, including decreased depression, anxiety, PTSD/trauma symptoms, anger, and body shame. It also promotes emotional resilience, happiness, and general well-being.[9] Among mental health professionals, it helps prevent occupational stress, burnout, and compassion fatigue.[10]

Self-compassion can also help us cope with the unavoidable suffering of illness. A 2020 review of 19 studies looking at the effect of self-compassion on psychosocial and clinical outcomes in medically ill patients. Ishita Misurya, Pranata Misurya, and Anirban Dutta found that self-compassion was associated with lower levels of patient anxiety, depression and stress, and an improvement in a range of medical outcomes.[11]

Self-compassion seems to be particularly useful in reducing feelings of threat and distress, resulting in a slowing of the heart rate, lowering of blood pressure, and an overall decrease in stress hormones. In turn, this leads to improvements in immune system functioning, better emotion regulation, reduced inflammation, improvements in cardiovascular health, and higher overall health status. It comes as no surprise, then, that self-compassion contributes to well-being in the short term and leads to long-term health benefits and positive aging.[12]

Receiving Compassion from Others

As we have discussed, self-compassion is often met with resistance and can be difficult for people to embrace. A corollary of this is the difficulty people have in receiving compassion from others. People who want to become more compassionate often think of themselves as givers of compassion, without realizing the importance of also allowing others to be compassionate towards them when they are suffering.

The British psychologist Paul Gilbert talks about "fear of compassion" in his book entitled *Mindful compassion*. He and his colleagues find that instead of being an open vessel to receive compassion from others, many people drift into feelings of shame and self-criticism, believing they are not worthy of self-compassion or compassion from others. They can be frightened or embarrassed by kindness and compassion from others, resist tenderness, or view receiving compassion as a weakness.[13] Does this apply to you? If so, what comes to mind when you think about receiving compassion from others?

A colleague of ours from Japan elegantly captures the meaning and beauty of receiving compassion from others in times of suffering:

> When I was diagnosed with stomach cancer, many of my friends sent me their well wishes, hoping that I would navigate that period of time in the best possible way. They organized healing circles to send me their love and healing energy. They also sent me numerous things that would be helpful as I embarked on a new life with the new condition I found myself in after the surgery. In addition, they provided me with information and advice to equip me with knowledge and strategies to tackle the challenges that lay ahead. I felt a sense of companionship during those difficult moments, as their kindness and care were freely extended towards me. They didn't have to go to such lengths, but their actions were motivated by their love, friendship, and compassion towards me.

Compassion is not a cog in an economic system or a duty required to function in society; it is an essential aspect of our humanity that goes beyond mechanical necessity. Through this experience, I came to realize its profound significance. Moreover, I began to realize the interconnectedness of various aspects of life and how people continually support each other by simply carrying out their roles in society. This newfound understanding made me feel like I was also a part of this network of individuals and elements that form the world.

* * * *

At the end of the day, self-compassion and receiving compassion from others go hand in hand with self-love. One of our students said this quite elegantly when talking about her recent struggles with relationships. We asked her what would she tell friends or siblings if they were going through the same struggles, and here's what she said:

> I would tell them to be kind to themselves, to treat themselves with the same love and compassion they show others. I did the same for myself. Through this journey, I discovered that the greatest love story is the one you have with yourself ... This was my journey to finding love within myself, and I finally found happiness in the most unexpected place—within.

Notes

1 www.statista.com/statistics/509679/value-of-the-global-anti-aging-market/
2 Kempton, B. (2018). *Wabi sabi: Japanese wisdom for a perfectly imperfect life.* Harper-Collins, p. 3.
3 Li, Qing (2018). *Forest bathing: How trees can help you find health and happiness.* Penguin/Random House, p. 222.
4 Neff, K. D. & Beretvas, S. N. (2012). The role of self-compassion in romantic relationships. *Self and Identity.* DOI:10.1080/15298868.2011.639548.
5 Hashem, Z. & Zeinoun, P. (2020). Self-compassion explains less burnout among healthcare professionals. *Mindfulness, 11* (11), 2542–2551.
6 Neff. K. & Germer C. (2017). Self-compassion and psychological well-being. In E. M. Seppala (et al.) *The Oxford handbook of compassion science.* Oxford University Press, p. 376.
7 Dweck, C. (2006). *Mindset: The new psychology of success.* Random House.

8   Neely, M. E., Schallert, D. L., Mohammed, S. S., Roberts, R. M., & Chen, Y. (2009). Self-kindness when facing stress: The role of self-compassion, goal regulation, and support in college students' well-being. *Motivation and Emotion, 33* (1), 88–97. https://doi.org/10.1007/s11031-008-9119-8.
9   Bluth, K. & Neff K, D. (2019). New frontiers in understanding the benefits of self-compassion. *Self Identity, 17* (6): 605–608.
10 Crego et al. (2022). The benefits of self-compassion in mental health professionals: A systematic review of empirical research. *Sychol Res Behav Manag., 15*, 2599–2620.
11 Misurya, I., Misurya, P. Y., & Dutta, A. (2020). The effect of self-compassion on psychosocial and clinical outcomes in patients with medical conditions: A systematic review. *Cureus, 12* (10). doi: 10.7759/cureus.10998.
12 Phillips, W. & Ferguson, S. (2013). Self-compassion: A resource for positive aging. *The Journals of Gerontology, 68* (4), 529–539.
13 Gilbert, P. & Choden. (2014). *Mindful compassion: How the science of compassion can help you understand your emotions, live in the present, and connect deeply with others.* New Harbinger Publications.

References

www.statista.com/statistics/509679/value-of-the-global-anti-aging-market/
Bluth, K. & Neff, K. D. (2019). New frontiers in understanding the benefits of self-compassion. *Self Identity, 17* (6), 605–-608.
Crego et al. (2022). The benefits of self-compassion in mental health professionals: A systematic review of empirical research. *Sychol Res Behav Manag., 15*, 2599–2620.
Dweck, C. (2006). *Mindset: The new psychology of success.* Random House.
Gilbert, P. & Choden. (2014). *Mindful compassion: How the science of compassion can help you understand your emotions, live in the present, and connect deeply with others.* New Harbinger Publications.
Hashem, Z. & Zeinoun, P. (2020). Self-compassion explains less burnout among healthcare professionals. *Mindfulness, 11* (11), 2542–2551.
Kempton, B. (2018). *Wabi sabi: Japanese wisdom for a perfectly imperfect life.* HarperCollins, p. 3.
Li, Qing (2018). *Forest bathing: How trees can help you find health and happiness.* Penguin/ Random House, p. 222.
Misurya, I., Misurya, P. Y., & Dutta, A. (2020). The effect of self-compassion on psychosocial and clinical outcomes in patients with medical conditions: A systematic review. *Cureus, 12* (10). doi: 10.7759/cureus.10998.
Neely, M. E., Schallert, D. L., Mohammed, S. S., Roberts, R. M., & Chen, Y. (2009). Self-kindness when facing stress: The role of self-compassion, goal regulation, and support in college students' well-being. *Motivation and Emotion, 33* (1), 88–97. https://doi.org/10.1007/s11031-008-9119-8.
Neff, K. D. & Beretvas, S. N. (2012). The role of self-compassion in romantic relationships. *Self and Identity.* DOI:10.1080/15298868.2011.639548.
Neff. K. & Germer C. (2017). Self-compassion and psychological well-being. In E. M. Seppala (et al.) *The Oxford handbook of compassion science.* Oxford University Press, p. 376.
Phillips, W. & Ferguson, S. (2013). Self-compassion: A resource for positive aging. *The Journals of Gerontology, 68* (4), 529–539.

7
COMPASSION TOWARDS ALL LIVING THINGS

If every person on the planet could extend compassion from themselves to their friends and family, to other humans, and, ultimately, toward all living things, the world we live in would be quite different. Imagine for a moment a new world enveloped in kindness. A world where compassion and a focus on our common humanity prevails. All children would grow up feeling loved and cared for, we would treat those who are different or those who transgress with respect and concern, violence and war would be a thing of the past, and so on. Sign us up!

Sadly, such a world isn't likely to materialize anytime soon, as we are ruled by a host of competing motives that help us navigate our lives. At the most basic level, we are motivated to avoid pain and danger and pursue pleasure and reward. Our brains and bodies are wired to identify and respond to threats and danger to maximize our chance of survival. We also are wired to seek rewards and acquire things, from concrete necessities like food and shelter to more lofty rewards like finding our purpose and experiencing happiness and joy. If we live in threatening and dangerous contexts, as many people around the world do, our threat-avoidance motives are likely to prevail. In the same vein, if we live in a society that overvalues material wealth and success at all costs, our lives are likely to be governed by the unyielding pursuit of rewards. And even though we

DOI: 10.4324/9781003312437-9

also are wired to care and connect with others, this care and connection motivation too often takes a back seat to fear and reward.

In *Mindful Compassion*, psychologist Paul Gilbert writes about the challenge of these competing motives. Take a look at what he has to say.

> While some spiritual traditions have tried to focus us on universal love, forgiveness, and the brotherhood of humanity, these motives, noble as they are, run up against opposing motives that are about getting ahead, securing power, destroying our enemies, or behaving with excessive cruelty to those around us. Even today, thousands of people are suffering from the terrors of war and torture, starvation stalks the lives of millions, and human wealth is held be a small minority who are reluctant to share. Consequently, compassionate motives are up against an evolved mind that is riddled with conflicting motives and desires.[1]

We realize that these distinct motivations all are adaptive and that we are all human beings with good days and bad days traveling on the same evolutionary highway. We are not suggesting that you deactivate your fear or reward systems. Rather, our focus in this chapter is on how we can better activate our *care and connection system*, achieve the optimal balance across these motivations (thus helping ourselves *and* others), and extend our compassion reach toward all living beings. This is consistent with Buddhist philosophy, which hinges on the concept of balance, of taking the *Middle Way* to live a balanced and controlled life that does not cause pain or suffering to any living being.

Take a few moments to think about *balance* in your life, particularly as it relates to making space for compassion. Do you have enough room for caring and connection? Can you extend your compassionate reach beyond those closest to you?

Expanding Your Compassion Reach: The Seven Virtues

One important lesson we've learned is to be aware of suffering and have the desire to alleviate it, but also to know our own capacities and limits. This awareness includes what we are capable of doing, what we are willing to do, what is needed, what is most likely to be effective, and what can be most impactful. The seven virtues of highly compassionate people can help us nurture this awareness.

We've discussed how *mindfulness* provides a foundation for compassion. It involves paying attention in a non-judgmental way to the flow of our thoughts and feelings. Mindfulness sets the stage for compassion towards both the self and others by calming our minds, enhancing our attention and present moment awareness, stimulating our care and connection system, and providing us with ample space to set our intentions. But mindfulness alone is not enough. Imagine being vividly aware of someone's trigger points and using this awareness to inflict harm rather than prevent it. Mindfulness must be coupled with other virtues to create a bridge to compassion.

Self-awareness allows us to know what we are capable of doing to help others. We all have certain strengths, gifts, or resources we can share with others. Your strength may be the ability to listen to someone else without judgment. Or it might be your ability to write compelling stories that move people towards empathy and kindness. Or you might have access to large sums of money that can help people in times of need.

Self-awareness also is critical in knowing what you are willing to do. Remember, the key is to achieve *balance* between your needs and desires and the needs and desires of others, to live in *harmony* with others. Some people choose to live a very simple life and give generously to needy groups and causes, while others want more for themselves and give very little. This is a personal decision, but in most all cases there is more you can do. Keep in mind, there are many ways to give to others. Even a kind word is a gift in a time of need.

Finally, self-awareness can help you recognize your limits and boundaries so you don't overextend yourself. As we will discuss in Chapter 8, we run the risk of compassion overload when suffering takes up too much space in our life. The world can often seem overwhelming, with suffering everywhere. Sometimes we just need to change the channel for a while and reflect on the kindness and goodness that surrounds us. This brings us to *gratitude*. We find that we need to consistently refocus on the good and appreciate the beauty around us. In doing so, we can bring light into darkness. If all we see is gloom and doom around us, it becomes much more difficult to harness the positive energy and light inside of us and share it with others.

Perspective-taking and *empathy* help us expand our compassion reach by tuning us in to what others feel and what they need. Have you ever done something that you thought would be helpful to others only to realize that it wasn't what they wanted or needed? Perhaps you even inadvertently offended them? We certainly have. Simply put, it's too easy to assume that other people need the same thing as you. We both tend to be problem-solvers; we try to fix things. But we have realized that sometimes all people want is an empathetic listener, regardless of whether you can or will help them solve the problem.

Kindness and *altruism* go hand in hand with mindfulness and self-awareness, like wings on a bird. They provide us with a moral compass that guides our actions from a perch of love and concern to help others. As we mentioned in Chapter 5, being kind and helpful can be as simple as picking up something someone dropped on the floor, saying a few kind words, or just taking time to acknowledge someone's presence. Try it out—let someone you usually walk right by know you see them by asking their name or thanking them for what they do. Thank the cleaner in a public restroom for doing a great job. Talk to someone who is asking for money on the street; ask what their name is and take a few minutes to listen to their story. Try to make a new connection, however small, with at least three people you don't know next week. Expand your circle of influence to as many people as you can on any given day—or better yet, every day!

You'll be surprised at the joy and happiness you can create with just a few words.

Figure 7.1 Our friend taking time to chat with a street artist in Santiago, Chile.
Source: © Nancy Guerra and Kirk R. Williams

Extending Compassionate Thoughts, Feelings, and Actions

Think for a few minutes about your own compassion reach. Consider the diagram below as your circle of influence, places where you are most likely to have a direct impact. Let's say you're at the center of this circle of influence. How many rings are there around you? Who's in these rings? How do you extend compassion towards the people in those rings?

Next, let's narrow our focus to the four rings below: People you love and care about, people in groups you belong to, people you work or go to school with, and acquaintances or people you sometimes interact with. These are all people whose paths cross yours in some fashion. Still, is it easier to extend compassion in some of these circles than in others?

Now, think about those whose paths *don't* cross yours or people you hold in contempt. Is it harder to extend compassion in these circles? If you are like most of us, extending compassion is easier for those you love and are closest to, like your family and friends. It is also easier to extend compassion to people who are like you and belong to the same social groups (or at least the social groups you identify with).

Throughout this book, we have noted the limits of empathy, specifically that it is easiest to extend to one's own social group but much harder to extend beyond. Similarly, it's hardest to extend compassion towards people you don't know or identify with. And it's particularly hard towards those you hold in contempt.

Oftentimes, we don't think about or grasp all the suffering around us, particularly if we don't see it every day. We go about our business avoiding danger, pursuing pleasure, and (hopefully) being kind to those we care

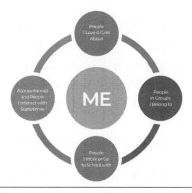

Figure 7.2 Your circle of influence.
Source: © Nancy Guerra and Kirk R. Williams

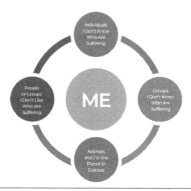

Figure 7.3 Beyond your circle of influence.
Source: © Nancy Guerra and Kirk R. Williams

about, but we neglect all the suffering beyond that. Sometimes it takes an epiphany to realize the harm we cause or allow to happen beyond our immediate circle of influence and then commit our lives to stopping it. A friend we met in the Stanford Compassion Cultivation Teacher Training Program, Lobsang Norbu, who left his job as a top chef to become a Buddhist monk, shared with us the moment that changed his life:

> The pivotal moment in my life came at the peak of my chef career. I worked in big resorts and small luxury restaurants, including one that was Michelin-starred. After working in the Caribbean for five years, I returned to Amsterdam and was working in a successful restaurant that featured a lot of seafood dishes, like lobster, oysters, and crab. The crab soup required me to sift through hundreds of live crabs to pick out the dead ones before I would fry them with chopped vegetables and flambée them with Cognac. I did things like that on a daily basis and never gave it a second thought.
>
> Then, one day, I suddenly was able to experience the world through the eyes of a lobster. It was a vivid and direct experience, as if it was me going to be boiled alive. I could not go back. I quit my job and never looked back. I thought, This animal is alive, it can feel pain. It doesn't want to die. *Just like me*. I knew all of that, but it meant nothing. Until that day. One moment of empathy changed all of that. Suddenly, I saw: This being is alive! It doesn't want to die! It can sense pain! *Just like me!*

We are both animal lovers, and we are particularly in tune with the harm we cause animals. Recently, we began working with a horse center in Colorado that takes in rescued horses and trains volunteers to work with them so they can be adopted. The neglect and cruelty we've seen is both astonishing and heartbreaking. But the joy we experience seeing horses learn to trust humans and connect emotionally and physically with them is amazing.

What about compassion for the planet? Take a moment to think about all the ways we harm the planet. Humans cause destruction in the form of plastics, pollution, fossil fuels, deforestation, overpopulation, waste, and so much more. We literally are killing the Earth and ourselves in the process.

What keeps us from extending compassion to the planet? To begin with, we have grown accustomed to the ease of living. We have a false sense of security because we recycle our bottles and bring our own bags to the market. But did you know that even when we recycle our plastic water bottles, 80% of them end up in landfills? What's more, huge amounts of oil are required to produce these plastic bottles, making them one of the greatest contributors to pollution.

In other cases, the process of destruction can seem slow or outside our realm of sight. If you live in Arizona, you don't have much direct experience with glaciers melting in Greenland. Whether you notice it or not, the damage we are causing is consequential and unprecedented. For example, the *Living Planet Report 2020* reports that 75% of the Earth's ice-free land has already been significantly changed by human activity,

Figure 7.4 Willow, the mini horse at the horse center.
Source: © Nancy Guerra and Kirk R. Williams

and almost 90% of our wetlands have been lost, with freshwater habitats suffering the greatest damage.

Sadly, there is money to be made through exploitation, and big business often values profits and growth over the health and well-being of both people and our planet. Have you heard of *extractivism*? A recent report released by The Ford Foundation, called *Building power in crisis: Women's responses to extractivism*, discusses not only the impact of massive extractions (mining, logging, drilling, etc.) on Earth, but how those extractions harm Indigenous peoples who suffer from degradation, poor water quality, and increased violence, which particularly impacts women and girls.

We are often reminded that everything is interconnected. Harm to someone or something causes harm to everything else in its ecosystem. We know this can get overwhelming. We also know that we all can and must do more. A good way to start is by extending compassionate thoughts and feelings to others and to all living beings.

Extending Compassionate Thoughts and Feelings

We have talked a lot in this book about the importance of translating compassionate wishes into compassionate actions. If we are to end suffering, we must work harder and work consistently towards our goal. Still, our actions largely are limited to our circle of influence, which for most of us is relatively small. In contrast, our thoughts and feelings have no boundaries. They are a very good place to begin.

We know that perceived similarity with others increases our empathic concern and motivation for action. We also know that failing to recognize our similarities and instead focusing on our differences leads to indifference at best and destruction at worst. That is where embracing our common humanity is an important first step. Just as Lobsang Norbu realized that all living things were ***just like him***, we realize that we all want to be free from suffering. Just as we wish to be happy, so do others. Just as we wish to be free from suffering, so do others.

How can you bring a ***just like me*** attitude into your thoughts and feelings on a daily basis? For starters, you can try as much as possible to keep that thought in the forefront of your mind, particularly when you are annoyed, angry, or upset with someone. There are also different visualizations and meditations you can use to help you access this mindset. The key is in finding what works best for you to access and harness your most compassionate spirit. Here is a soothing visualization technique you can use.

> Start with your basic mindfulness practices of rhythmic breathing and settling your mind. Now, take some time to recall an image that soothes you. This could be a color that conveys warmth, a place you love that conveys peace and tranquility, or a compassionate image or deity that you view as the embodiment of everything kind and good. Allow this image to flow through you, soothe you, and enter your soul. Let this image fade away, but try to keep it with you in some form for the rest of the day, reflected in your facial expressions, body posture, thoughts, feelings, and actions.

Guided meditations for embracing common humanity are helpful. These typically begin by calling to mind someone or something you hold dear, then someone you know of but don't interact with, then someone you find difficult, and finally all these people together. In all situations, the objective is to embrace what you have in common and how you all want to be happy and free from suffering. You'll see that it's quite easy to do with someone you love.

A more challenging meditation involves actively imagining you are taking away suffering from others as you breathe in, and that you are sending out happiness as you breathe out. This method is called *tonglen*, meaning giving and receiving. The universality of suffering allows you to connect with others by imagining you are taking away their suffering as you breathe in and replacing it with your love and compassion as you breathe out. The beauty of tonglen is that it can be done anywhere and for anyone, including for the planet. In a sense, it is quite similar to prayer, although instead of praying to a deity who suffered for all of us and asking the deity to convey happiness towards someone else, you become the vessel to receive this suffering and transform it into hope and light for both yourself and others.

To be honest, when we first tried tonglen we found it difficult to imagine breathing in suffering—a very common experience. We can be attentive to others' suffering and think about who we want to spread loving-kindness to, but we found it easier to breathe in energy from the forest, other people, the universe—to breathe in goodness—and to breathe out our wishes to spread this goodness beyond ourselves. However, as we learned more about tonglen we understood that it was really a practice of *transforming* suffering into well-being, much like an air filter takes in dusty air and puts out fresher air. Think of a somewhat troubling image (the suffering) that you can transform with your breath into lightness (well-being), whether this be a dark sky into sunlight or heavy, hot air into a cool breeze.

Tonglen can also transform you and help you cultivate your natural mercy towards self and others. It helps you open your heart to its natural state of warmth, spaciousness, and kindness.

You can begin with yourself, focus on a specific person or persons, or think about suffering on a larger scale. We find it most rewarding to use tonglen for a specific person who is suffering, someone we can touch and connect with and transfer our positive energy into their body. There are many guided meditations for practicing tonglen and loving-kindness available online. We hope you find the technique that works best for you.

Extending Compassionate Action

Translating compassionate motivation into compassionate action requires awareness of your gifts, your circle of influence, and what you are comfortable doing. It also requires knowing what is best to do across different

Figure 7.5 Out of the darkness comes the light. Sunrise over Utah heading east on Interstate 70.
Source: © Nancy Guerra and Kirk R. Williams

situations and contexts, that is, knowing the best way to provide the most help to alleviate suffering and promote happiness and joy in yourself and others. Take a moment to think about your *gifts*. What are you able and willing to do to help make the world a better place, whether in small or grand ways? What are your biggest gifts?

Now, think about all the people and places you can impact. This includes:

- People you care deeply about.
- People you regularly interact with in social groups, at work, at school, or in your neighborhood.
- Acquaintances and people you interact with sometimes.
- People or groups *you don't know* who are suffering.
- Animals or the planet in distress.
- People or groups *you don't like* who are suffering.

Think about and write down all the ways you **currently** have an impact in each of these contexts and the gifts you share. Then think about and write down actions you **could take and are willing to take** to make a difference. Select one or two things in the **could do** list to try each week.

Next, let's think about **effective altruism**. The basic idea in this thought is that to help most effectively, we must use both our hearts and our minds. In other words, it's not enough to simply *want* to do good; it's just as important to find the best way to help the greatest number of people and to focus on those who are suffering the most.

The effective altruism movement arose from the realization that many attempts to do good instead fail or even cause harm, while others can be extremely effective. The movement also helps people harness their gifts and use them to promote good. For example, one might choose a career based on the amount of good it can do or the amount of money it provides to donate more to good causes.

On the one hand, it clearly makes sense to give money to the charity with the greatest impact, and there are many charity watchdog websites that help you evaluate their effectiveness. On the other hand, your motivation may not be based on effectiveness. For example, you could say that the Make-A-Wish Foundation is not a very effective use of money in terms of finding a cure for disease or alleviating long-term suffering. But for the children who participate, it is the experience of a lifetime. There have also been criticisms that focusing on charity to solve the world's problems takes society's eye off of trying to make more meaningful changes to deeper, systemic sociopolitcal issues. Our take-home message is that we all must find our own path, our own journey of compassion, and then decide for ourselves how we can be most impactful.

Keep in mind that doing good doesn't always have to result in some immediate effect. Our actions have a ripple effect on those around us. In turn, those people have an effect on those around them, and so on. The impact of what we do can live on long beyond us. Irving Yalom, a well-known existential psychiatrist, talks about the "rippling effect" in his book, *Staring at the sun: Overcoming the dread of death*. He contends this rippling effect occurs through concentric circles of influence we create that work just like ripples in a pond, continuing to be felt by others long after we are gone.[2]

What will you leave behind that ripples out to others? What more can you do to create ripples that spread compassion and joy for future generations?

Compassion Across Contexts

In Chapter 2, we discussed how we are born to care, how compassion gives us an evolutionary advantage. But even if we are wired to behave in certain ways, different contexts can make any behavior more or less likely, and perhaps even nonexistent. Think for a moment about our biological instinct to fight (fight or flight). We are all pre-wired to use aggression, but different contexts make this behavior more or less likely. You can imagine a context where aggression is required to survive (for instance, on the battlefield), but you can also imagine a context where there is no need for aggression or where it is actively discouraged.

The same goes for compassion. Can you imagine what schools, corporations, and communities would look like if they were organized to encourage compassion? And because compassion so often takes a back seat to our desire to avoid threat and seek rewards, it is even more important to structure these places intentionally to call for compassion.

There have been a number of collaborative efforts to bring compassion into diverse settings. These efforts operate at many different levels, such as training individuals in compassion-related virtues. For example, over the past few decades, social-emotional learning programs have become mainstream in many schools. In some schools, these programs also are part of a larger, holistic effort to promote wellness through teaching, resources, and opportunities. For example, the *Compassionate Schools Project* (www. compassionschools.org) is an extensive, seven-year-spanning project in 45 schools that has focused specifically on developing compassionate schools.

At a broader level, communities mobilized to build services and implement policies that embody compassion and help prevent suffering. The *Charter for Compassion* provides an umbrella for communities to organize for the collective benefit of all residents. As Karen Armstrong, founder of this global movement, says, "A compassionate city is an uncomfortable city! A city that is uncomfortable when anyone is homeless or hungry. Uncomfortable if every child isn't loved and given rich opportunities to grow and thrive. Uncomfortable when, as a community, we don't treat our neighbors as we would wish to be treated."[3]

In the corporate world, the concept of *stakeholder capitalism* has taken hold. A notable event occurred at the 2020 World Economic Forum in Davos, which opened with the theme of "Stakeholders for a Cohesive and Sustainable World." In essence, this reflects a shift away from *shareholder capitalism*, a practice that focuses on generating the greatest profit for shareholders. Instead of focusing only on profits, stakeholder capitalism creates benefits for all stakeholders, including customers, employees, suppliers, communities, and shareholders. Businesses are viewed as an important force for good. A compelling testimony of how stakeholder capitalism is seeping into businesses is the rapid rise in the number of B Corporations in the world. B Corporations (B stands for benefit) are mission-driven companies that balance profit with other values, particularly social and environmental concerns. As of early 2023, there were over 6,000 B Corporations in more than 150 industries across more than 80 countries. That number represents close to a 50% increase in certified B Corporations since 2020.

Advocates for compassion also are organizing into global networks of action. For example, the Global Compassion Coalition (https:// globalcompassioncoalition.org) wants to stimulate change at a global level. In more specific terms, they wish to build a new world based on compassion—a world where all people can thrive and prosper.

Figure 7.6 Explora Chile is a sustainable tourism B Corporation dedicated to environmental preservation.
Source: © Nancy Guerra and Kirk R. Williams

* * * *

As we have seen in this chapter, there are many ways to broaden your compassion reach. At the end of the day, the best way to extend compassion to others is to become the embodiment of compassion. This means being compassionate with yourself and others using your mind, body, and heart. Compassion becomes a way of being or an orientation to living that permeates all aspects of your life.

Being compassionate requires bringing positivity and calmness into your life through meditation, mindfulness, and any other techniques or strategies that work for you. It also involves intentional reflective practices that keep you grounded in your vision of a more compassionate world, a world where we embrace our common humanity at every turn.

Here is a brief exercise you can try whenever you want to remind yourself of the deep connections you have with all living things.

Think of someone you share no similarities with. Next, think about or make a list of all the things you actually *do* share in common with that person. (For starters, remember that you share 99% of your DNA.) Now reflect on these commonalities. Do they make you see this person in a new light? Repeat this exercise when you are tempted to exclude someone or when you come across someone you think is different than you.

Notes

1 Gilbert, P. and Choden (2014). *Mindful compassion: How the science of compassion can help you understand your emotions, life in the present, and connect deeply with others*. New Harbinger Publications, p. 34.
2 Yalom, I. D. (2009). *Staring at the sun: Overcoming the fear of death*. Jossey-Bass.
3 Karen Armstrong. *Charter for Compassion*. www.charterforcompassion.org

References

Armstrong, Karen. *Charter for Compassion*. www.charterforcompassion.org
Gilbert, Paul and Choden (2014). *Mindful compassion: How the science of compassion can help you understand your emotions, life in the present, and connect deeply with others*. New Harbinger Publications, p. 34.
Yalom, I. D. (2009). *Staring at the sun: Overcoming the fear of death*. Jossey-Bass.

PART III
MOVING FORWARD

8
BARRIERS TO COMPASSION

We've covered a lot of ground so far regarding how to live a life of compassion. We began with the *what* of compassion, including the meaning and manifestations of suffering, and the connection between compassion and preventing or alleviating suffering. We then discussed the *why* of compassion. We talked about the evolutionary advantages and the benefits of living a compassion-driven life. We just finished the *how* of compassion. This includes preparing yourself for compassion by decluttering, reframing, and setting your intentions. This clears the path for building the seven virtues of highly compassionate people. We then looked at how to apply this to practicing self-compassion and compassion towards all living beings.

We now turn to the challenges of bringing compassion into your life. In particular, we attempt to answer the following question: What stands in the way of compassion? Remember from Chapter 1 that compassion requires an attentiveness to suffering. We can't do much to prevent or alleviate suffering if we are unaware of its multiple manifestations. Once we become aware of suffering, however, compassion does not necessarily follow. Other factors come into play that may interfere with or literally block a compassionate response, even if we are aware of and emotionally motivated to do something about suffering. We refer to such factors as *barriers to compassion*.

DOI: 10.4324/9781003312437-11

There are two main sets of barriers. The first is linked to feeling over-whelmed by suffering. We call this *compassion overload*. This can occur when you are simply worn out from being the caregiver and from always having to be compassionate, which we refer to as *compassion fatigue*. Overload also can occur when suffering is so overwhelming that it seems impossible to do anything to help (like a raging river that washes away your ability to swim against the current). This is called *compassion collapse*. Most of the social and behavioral science research focuses on these components of compassion overload.

The second set of barriers we refer to as *compassion roadblocks*. Simply put, these are features of everyday life that are not compassion friendly, meaning they block access to compassionate responses. Such features involve a host of factors we all contend with as we go about our lives. Some are less obvious; for example, social norms that dictate when compassion is or is not appropriate. Other roadblocks are part of the circumstances of our lives; for example, dangerous contexts direct our attention to staying safe and getting through each day. Yet another set of roadblocks occurs within us, whether that means wandering thoughts or explosive emotions that divert our attention away from compassion.

Compassion Overload: Fatigue and Collapse

Compassion Fatigue

Imagine you have the full-time responsibility of taking care of a loved one who is suffering from a terminal illness. Because of your loving attach-ment to this person, you want to be there, meeting daily needs that arise. Doing so can be gratifying, especially if your caregiving efforts are reduc-ing pain and improving their remaining quality of life. However, your caregiving behavior undoubtedly will take a toll on your own well-being. If nothing else, your energy level is likely to dissipate, meaning you'll feel tired and drained. Witnessing a loved one struggle with a terminal illness and accepting that the end is near in itself is stressful. At some point, you feel like a "time out" is necessary to recover your physical and mental health. Yet, taking a break will likely come with feelings of guilt, as you're not tending to your loved one's needs.

This kind of situation is infused with a complicated mix of emotions, which can wear you out no matter how much you love this person and want to help. The physical, mental, and emotional exertion drains your tank, so to speak. Like working out to become physically fit, you can't keep doing it endlessly. Your muscles get tired and require rest to rejuvenate. Unfortunately, some situations don't give you the time to do so, often leading to compassion fatigue.

Compassion fatigue is a particularly pressing issue for professionals in the caregiving business, from health care providers to human service workers, who have the full-time responsibility of taking care of suffering patients or clients. Their jobs require them to be compassionate virtually every day. That kind of professional responsibility is a heavy load that can and does lead to professional burnout. The COVID-19 pandemic, for instance, led to widespread compassion fatigue. The massive number of cases and deaths put inordinate pressure on health care providers, with hundreds of thousands of workers leaving their jobs due to burnout. A report from Smartlinx, a healthcare workforce platform (www.smartlinx.com/), shows that the COVID-19 pandemic was listed as the number one reason health care providers left their jobs, with one in five quitting since the beginning of the pandemic.

It's not surprising, then, that much (if not most) of the research and discussion about compassion fatigue focuses on professionals in the caregiving business. Some researchers have tried to predict who will develop compassion fatigue and who will be resilient in the face of ongoing suffering. Do you have any ideas about what factors increase or decrease the likelihood of compassion fatigue (and what might be useful for you if you experience such fatigue)? In one study, Charles and Kathleen Figley found that the greater the time professionals were exposed to patient suffering, the greater their compassion fatigue. On the other hand, those who were able to detach in some fashion reported less fatigue. Strategies that worked best included taking physical and mental breaks from suffering, engaging in self-care, drawing on the inherent satisfaction of helping others, and relying on support from colleagues, friends, and family. These strategies fostered resilience to compassion fatigue.[1]

In sum, whether you're dealing with an enduring compassionate response to the suffering of loved ones or the prolonged exposure to suffering experienced as a professional caregiver, suffering can become overwhelming. It can drain personal resources to the point that an effective expression of compassion is weakened, maybe even precluded. This form of compassion overload results from intense, direct exposure to suffering, withering our ability to respond compassionately. The best response is to find a way to take a break. There are also a number of resources available online to help you cope. We particularly like this video by Kristen Neff, which you can find on YouTube: www.youtube.com/watch?v=jJ9w GfwE-YE.

Compassion Collapse

Hopefully, we now have a shared understanding that compassion involves recognition of suffering and the desire or motivation to prevent or alleviate suffering. We also have a shared understanding that suffering takes many forms and extends from ourselves to others, which includes those close to us and those far away. With that in mind, consider this question: Will your compassionate response to suffering increase with the extent of the suffering? In other words, are you more likely to respond with compassion as the number of people harmed increases, the size of the disaster grows, or the overall level of suffering increases?

We've actually posed this question to many of our students and friends, and their answer usually is "yes," meaning greater suffering leads to greater compassion. That makes intuitive sense. If more people are impacted by some form of suffering, we'd assume that our emotional (how horrified we are) and, perhaps, behavioral response (what we'd do about it) would be intensified. Saying "yes" also makes sense because we likely think we *ought* to feel or act more compassionately when the human trauma is extensive.

But what is so intriguing is that research actually suggests the opposite. Studies find that as the number of victims in a crisis increases, compassionate emotions and behavior actually decrease. This holds across different studies using different methodologies, as C. Daryl Cameron reported in a recent review. He sums up this paradox by noting that "Compassion appears to break down exactly when it is needed the most."[2] Given these research findings, a reasonable question to ask is this: Why does it happen?

One possible explanation is that we don't have the bandwidth to process extensive suffering mentally, emotionally, or behaviorally. It's simply easier to process a single person with a visible face than lots of unrecognizable people, especially if they are far removed from us. Why do you think charitable organizations ask you to sponsor a hungry child, including a picture of the child, rather than donate to fight world hunger, even though approximately 19,000 people die of hunger globally each day? It's because you can relate to one hungry child, especially if you see his or her sad and drawn face, more easily than you can relate to 19,000 people dying each day from hunger. This is true despite the fact that the collective catastrophe is greater than one child's experience.

As one further example, think back to our discussion of empathy in Chapter 5. It's a lot easier to connect with how others are feeling when we know the other person, such as a family member or close friend. Trying to empathize with large unknown groups, even if they are experiencing widespread suffering, taxes our emotional capacity. We may sympathize with such suffering and open our hearts to it, but we also likely feel it's beyond our capability to do anything about it.

In sum, unlike compassion fatigue, which results from direct and prolonged exposure to the suffering of those we are caring for, compassion collapse is more indirect. Extensive suffering is significantly more difficult to wrap our heads and hearts around, especially when it involves multiple people and widespread destruction in distant places. However, both compassion fatigue and collapse have this in common: they take up too much space in our lives, resulting in mental and emotional overload and even interfering with effective compassionate action.

Compassion Roadblocks

Normative Standards for Behavior

Figure 8.1 Roadblocks come in many forms.
Source: © Nancy Guerra and Kirk R. Williams

Think about how much of what you do is governed by norms that provide guidelines for how you should think, feel, and act in different settings. Although these guidelines vary across cultures and historical times, they nevertheless create strong expectations for appropriate behavior, some of which can interfere with compassionate responding. Family or family-like contexts, for example, include expectations for what it means to be a wife, husband, or partner, how they should treat each other, and, if children are involved, how parent-child relations should unfold. Academic contexts are infused with expectations for administrators, teachers, professors, staff, and students, particularly when it comes to their respective responsibilities and how they should relate to each other. Places of work have shared expectations for who does what, who's in charge, and when tasks should be completed. Different stages in the life course from infancy, childhood, and adolescence to adulthood and senior living involve normative expectations about age-appropriate behaviors.

Suffice it to say that virtually every social setting in which we participate has roles, responsibilities, and shared expectations for what we're supposed to do. And these features of our lives existed before we ever came on the scene. That said, normative expectations for behavior are not fixed—they can change over time and vary from place to place. Moreover, people in any given social setting may interpret these standards differently, which, in turn, can influence their mental, emotional, and behavioral responses to what's happening around them.

How do you think normative standards for behavior might create a roadblock for compassion? A good example we can think of involves norms for gender-appropriate behavior. Chew on this question next: What does it mean to be a man or a woman? We recognize this question raises complex and controversial issues. It's not just about differences in internal or external genitalia, the production of sperm versus eggs, chromosome composition (XY versus XX chromosomes), or differential levels of estrogen, progesterone, or testosterone. Of course, that's all part of it, but these and other characteristics indicate *biological sex* differences.

Enter gender identity. This issue goes beyond biological sex categorization. Here we enter the world of cultural ideals pertaining to femininities and masculinities. We state these terms in plural form because no uniform, fixed definition of femininity or masculinity exists. That's part of the controversy. The attributes reflecting the culturally ideal images for masculinity and femininity vary historically and geographically. They also vary across different subgroups within a society or across the world's population at any given point in time. Further, what it means to be a man or a woman varies across the course of one's life. For example, a teenage boy may define and demonstrate masculinity quite differently than a young married man who has children or a retired senior man who has adult children and grandchildren.

Given the diversity of meanings across age groups, historical periods, and societies, femininities and masculinities are not biologically based but are infused in the culture of the place, subgroup, and time. In short, the meaning of femininity and masculinity is socially constructed. Michael Kimmel, a retired Distinguished Professor of Sociology specializing in Gender Studies, notes how sex is biological, but gender is socially constructed. Gender takes shape only within specific social and cultural contexts.[3] Although he acknowledges that masculinity and femininity mean different things to different groups of people at different times, he points out that some definitions are considered more esteemed and dominant than others. Raewyn Connell, an Australian Sociologist, talks about hegemonic masculinity, a culturally idealized form of dominant masculinity in a network of gender inequality.[4]

Although we recognize the complex and controversial issues swirling about sex and gender, we choose not to engage the swirl. Instead, we choose to illustrate how living up to cultural ideals of masculinity can impede living a compassionate life. We do so by discussing how traditional or conventional characteristics of masculinity, Kimmel's dominant model, stand in the way of achieving a compassionate life.

Let's begin by reviewing some traditional or conventional cultural ideals of what it means to be a man. Think of the various characteristics that are often attributed to masculinity. "Real men" are stoic. They should stand tall under all circumstances without becoming emotional, whether that means avoiding expressions of pain or sorrow, pleasure or joy. They should be independent and self-reliant, resulting in a reluctance to make meaningful connections with others, particularly outside one's immediate social circle, or to seek help in accomplishing tasks or tending to personal needs. Doing so would be a sign of vulnerability and weakness. Indeed, those outside the immediate social circle are seen as competitors the man must overcome in his incessant pursuit of scarce resources and personal achievement. Self-worth is buttressed by besting others.

This pursuit results in an orientation to the external world, with the internal world of contemplation and emotion pushed aside. As Ed Adams and Ed Frauenheim discuss in their book, *Reinventing masculinity: The liberating power of compassion and connection*, this dominant form of masculinity, what they call confined masculinity, tends to wall men off emotionally, with the result being an unawareness of the needs of the soul or psyche. Moreover, the intense competition for scarce resources creates anxiety and about getting enough of whatever is being pursued.[5]

Here's one last characteristic we'll mention. "Real men" recoil from anything that smacks of femininity, such as nurturance, sensitivity, cooperativeness, emotional expressiveness, understanding, empathy, and support for the well-being of others. As Michael Kimmel notes, models of masculinity and femininity are relational, meaning they are developed in contrast to each other.[6] This is reflected in a football coach, disappointed with his players' lack of aggressiveness, saying, "You're playing like a bunch of women!"

Granted, this characterization of masculinity doesn't encompass all dimensions of masculinity, and many might quibble with those mentioned above. Even if we had an exhaustive list of culturally idealized forms of manhood, not all men (or women, for that matter) would necessarily identify with those forms or incorporate them into their way of living. Nonetheless, our characterization illustrates the central point. Internalizing such a culturally idealized rendition of masculinity into one's identity interferes with living a compassionate life. This form of manhood squashes caring and connection emotions and mobilizes feelings of fear and anger or the unrelenting pursuit of power, domination, and control.

It's difficult to imagine that an uncritical acceptance of this form of masculinity would facilitate the seven virtues of compassionate people. Extreme competitiveness and deflection do not make fertile ground for mindfulness or deep self-awareness. Endless acquiring diverts attention from the present moment and prevents savoring gratitude. The self-focused drive to overcome and succeed leaves little room for perspective taking or concern (empathy) for the well-being of others. Winning at any cost is surely not a manifestation of kindness or a desire to give to others (altruism).

To be clear, we're not blaming men for creating suffering for others or for the general indifference to suffering that seems to be widespread globally. In fact, Richard Reeves' recent book, *Of boys and men: Why the modern male is struggling, why it matters, and what to do about it,* documents how men themselves are suffering in multiple ways because of structural changes in society and the idea that they must live up to a less than positive vision of masculinity. This suffering extends from despair-related deaths like drug overdoses or suicide to falling behind in education and the labor market, to fathers losing touch with their children.[7]

We do contend, however, that abiding by a culturally corrosive form of masculinity can derail compassion. The good news is that from childhood to adulthood, boys and men can be socialized to critically evaluate the normative expectations of who they are and what they do. They can then choose to be different. And, since masculinity is a cultural rather than biological feature, it can be modified. We can, then, discard elements antithetical to compassion and blend in those that champion compassion.

Compassion-Unfriendly Contexts

Life is not lived in a vacuum. We're not isolated individuals who roll around like marbles in a jar. We are interconnected, and we experience life in various social settings, ranging from close family and friendships to neighborhoods, schools, and workplaces, all of which are embedded in the larger political, economic, and world order. Such ever-expanding social settings influence how we think, feel, and act. Each context provides resources (or the lack thereof), opportunities (whether limited or expansive), and collective experiences that impact our daily lives. These interconnected external influences draw on our inner world; specifically, the three emotional regulation systems discussed in the previous chapter. Sometimes, a certain context can evoke care and connection thoughts and emotions, which heighten our attention to suffering and motivate us to do something about it. Other times, contexts arouse fear and anxiety or relentless yearning for accomplishment, which blunts our sensitivity to suffering and its prevention or alleviation. Let's consider some examples.

Figure 8.2. A mother dove calmly sitting on her nest.
Source: © Nancy Guerra and Kirk R. Williams

Some contexts are supportive and facilitate the cultivation of compassion. For example, imagine a family with loving and nurturing relationships that live in a safe and affluent neighborhood. These relationships, buttressed by an enriched environment, can be the source of healthy and equally enriched support for day-to-day living. Such a family provides a context in which adult partners and children feel content, safe, and secure. In this setting, people can find solace and peaceful well-being, even in the face of a fast-paced, frenetic world.

Settings like these stimulate soothing emotions and affiliation—or what we call the caring and connection emotional regulation system. Emotions associated with this system calm us down, soften our anxiety and help us be more positive and gentle.[8] They also can mitigate the threat-based and resource-seeking emotions that can divert us from attending and responding to suffering compassionately. In short, loving and kind relationships, coupled with emotions linked to caring and interpersonal connections, enable a compassionate response to perceived suffering in ourselves and others.

However, other contexts are not so friendly to compassion. We've previously discussed how living under conditions of adversity and economic hardship can divert our attention from suffering. Even when we see it, we may not have the desire, capability, or opportunity for compassionate action. These contexts accentuate feelings of fear and anger, which are threat-based emotions, as well as the drive to acquire some form of success. The demands and constraints of such contexts simply dilute compassion as an orientation to living. Here's a couple more illustrative contexts that are not compassion friendly, one involving daily, life-threatening events, and the other involving intense competition that tramples both our care and connection emotions and our ability to live compassionately.

Military conflicts are an obvious context that block a compassionate response to suffering. They are deadly, threatening the lives of those in battle and the unfortunate civilians who become collateral casualties of lethal fighting. We've mentioned the Ukraine conflict in Chapter 1, noting the destruction and refugee crisis that now exists. Thousands of Ukrainian citizens have been killed or injured, and millions have been displaced either within the country or are now refugees out of the country. The death toll for Ukrainian and Russian troops is also staggering. In another military conflict, Sudan is in chaos because of two rival Sudanese generals fighting for power—one heading the nation's army, the other leading the paramilitary group Rapid Support Forces. The World Health Organization estimates that hundreds of civilians have been killed and tens of thousands of Sudanese civilians have fled by land or sea to neighboring countries.

Military conflicts like these create a context for people living within them that suppresses emotions of caring and connection, which facilitate compassion. Instead of creating those emotions, military conflicts elicit threat-based emotions such as fear, anger, and disgust. They also stimulate an emphasis on seeking resources for survival and defense. The context overwhelms the capacity for compassion even among the most well-intentioned people. No doubt, those living outside these settings may recognize this widespread suffering and open their hearts to send compassionate thoughts, wishes, and perhaps financial donations to assist those who suffer. Nonetheless, the immediate circumstances for those in the midst of the conflicts are dire and directly interfere with compassionate living.

Apart from settings filled with life-threatening violence, think about other contexts where marked competition prevails. What comes to mind? The options are wide-ranging because we live in a society where competition is the motor that drives almost everything. Children compete with each other for parental attention. Students compete with each other for class standing, popularity, athletic status, and so on. Workers compete with each other for productivity, pay increases, and promotions. Real estate agents compete with each other for listings and home sales. Businesses compete with each other for a larger market share. Drug cartels compete with each other for drug distribution routes, markets, and political influence. Religious organizations compete with each other for theological persuasion and believers. Political parties compete with each other for governmental power and control. Countries compete with each other for political and economic dominance in the world. And on and on. It's virtually impossible to think of a context untouched by competition. From interpersonal comparisons to international relations, our lives are replete with competition.

The issue, therefore, is not whether competition is present or absent in life's various social contexts. The issue is whether competition is so intense that it blunts our sensitivity to the suffering of ourselves and others. We become driven by the excitement to accomplish and acquire or by the fear of failure and panic to survive. And far too often, whether intended or not, we become jaded to the consequences of intensified striving for success. Fueled by competition—our excessive drive to achieve, acquire, dominate, and control—our need to win at any cost can numb us to suffering.

In turn, indifference and disregard surface within us. At the extreme, we create suffering for ourselves. (For example, we work ourselves to the bone so that we develop physical and mental health problems.) On top of that, we create suffering for others. (For example, we undermine someone else's honest efforts for our own self-gain, whether that means cheating on exams, insider trading on Wall Street, or even the intimidation or assassination of political opposition.)

In short, contexts with heightened scarcity, adversity, life-threatening violence, and destruction or intensified competition suppress caring and connection emotions. Instead, they spark feelings of fear, anger, and despair or the unrelenting pursuit of self-aggrandizement, power, domination, and control. Living a compassionate life in such contexts is a challenge to say the least.

Emotions, Thoughts, and Motivations That Interfere With Compassion

Have you ever tried to sit still, calm down, and let your body and mind rest? These are important things to do to achieve mindfulness. However, our multitasking and high-energy lifestyles often crowd out such attempts. Even when we *do* try, we often get fidgety, our minds floating from thought to thought like hummingbirds feeding in a flower garden. Paul Gilbert, a British clinical psychologist who founded Compassion Focused Therapy (CFT) and Compassion Mind Training (CMT), refers to these bouncing thoughts as attention hopping, where our mind wanders all over the place. We're sure that you, like most people, have experienced attention hopping. The problem is that attention hopping too often slides into rumination and brooding. When that happens, we can easily get stuck in a negative swirl, leading to depression and anxiety.

Here's another inheritance of being human. Have you ever walked down the street, and someone texting bumps into you? As professors on a large university campus, where students obsessively text while walking from class to class, we've experienced this many times. If this happened to you, how did you react? Did you calmly say, "Oh, excuse me. I must have gotten in your way." Or did anger kick in, causing you to say, "Get off your phone and watch where you're going!" Here's another example. Have you ever been in a restaurant or flying on a commercial jet and had someone, perhaps a server or a flight attendant, spill a drink on you? Again, how did you react? Were you understanding and forgiving? Or did you become irritated and react to the person as clumsy and incompetent?

Both of these scenarios are examples of unexpected happenings that catch us off guard. When they occur, we tend to react immediately with negative emotions (usually irritability, anger, and disgust), which literally take control of our attention, body, thinking, and behavior and trigger our threat-based emotional regulation system. This system of emotional regulation is part of our human inheritance, and it has historically kept us safe. It promoted self-protection by alerting us to danger and equipping us for rapid detection and response to that danger. Anger ignites aggressive responses, anxiety pushes us in the direction of avoidance or running away, and disgust leads us to get rid of or destroy the threat or danger. Such emotions are part of who we are; therefore, we must accept and learn how to manage them. We can't get rid of them, but we can learn to better manage them and decide the proper contexts to use them in. If we become more aware of these emotions and what triggers them, we can intentionally disengage them when they are not needed, thus paving the way for compassion.

Drive and resource-seeking emotions can also interfere with compassion. Once again, these are hardwired into our brains because they were important for acquiring resources and thus fostering survival and reproduction of the human species. Excitement around seeking and obtaining material possessions, financial resources, status, and power is the hallmark of this emotional regulation system. As we have discussed previously, such excitement is functional in our highly competitive social world. However, an obsession with accomplishment can result in an unregulated and even ruthless "winning at any cost" mindset, which leads us to trample over others in the pursuit of self-gain.

Unfortunately, that obsession often results in the denigration or dehumanization of those we seek to overcome, dominate, and control. In short, we can become insensitive and indifferent to the suffering of others, perhaps even creating that suffering in their lives. Think of the numerous casualties associated with the struggle for power between the national army and the paramilitary force in Sudan or the Russian invasion of Ukraine. Think also of the political struggles for power in the United States, which so often promotes polarization and extremism.

The point of this discussion is that humans have inherent characteristics that are vital to our well-being and survival as a species. However, those same characteristics, when untamed, can deaden our sensitivity to suffering and our desire to do anything about it. This latter point is crucial. Taming the mind and our emotions is vital for practicing mindfulness and cultivating compassion.

Taming doesn't mean fixing or mechanically managing our mind and emotions. It especially doesn't mean forcing out bad thoughts or emotions and bringing in good thoughts and emotions. Doing so involves a judgmental mental process, whereas mindfulness involves a non-judgmental and deliberate present-moment awareness of our thoughts and emotions as they unfold. It's like watching a movie and maintaining an accepting awareness that we're watching a movie. Learning to be accepting and present with our thoughts and emotions has been emphasized for centuries in the Buddhist tradition, as well as in more recent secular developments, such as in the work of John Kabat-Zinn (2009). He pioneered the therapeutic application of mindfulness, especially in dealing with chronic pain through a Mindfulness-Based Stress Reduction program.[9]

Figure 8.3 Be in tune with the rhythms of your life just like the rhythms of the waves breaking on shore.
Source: © Nancy Guerra and Kirk R. Williams

So, in the end, if meandering thoughts and the swirl of internal emotions carry you away at times, don't feel guilty or discouraged. You're only human. Trust that incorporating mindfulness as a way of living—as a daily disciplined practice—will help you orchestrate your internal world rather than having it orchestrate you.

* * * *

We included this chapter on barriers to compassion to acknowledge that life involves suffering, and that our attention and responsiveness *to* that suffering requires daily, disciplined practice. We never really arrive, so to speak; we just continue to set our intention and make every effort to orient ourselves to living a life of compassion.

And guess what? It's not easy. We often get overwhelmed by all the suffering in our lives, or we run into roadblocks that interfere with our attentiveness and compassionate responsiveness to suffering. Those roadblocks include adverse contexts of living, normative standards for behavior, or just the vicissitudes of daily life. By being aware of the barriers and roadblocks to compassion, we take one step closer to overcoming them.

Notes

1 Figley, C. R. & Figley, K. R. (2017). Compassion fatigue resilience. In E. M. Seppala et al. (eds). *The Oxford handbook of compassion science*. Oxford University Press, pp. 387–397.

2   Cameron, C. D. (2017). Compassion collapse: Why we are numb to numbers. In E. M. Seppala et al. (eds). *The Oxford handbook of compassion science.* Oxford University Press, pp. 262–271.
3   Kimmel, M. (2001) Masculinities and Femininities. In *International encyclopedia of the social and behavioral sciences).* Elsevier Science Ltd, pp. 9318–9321.
4   Connell, R. W. (1987). *Gender and power.* Stanford University Press.
5   Adams, E. M. & Frauenheim, E. (2020) *Reinventing masculinity: The liberating power of compassion and connection.* Berrett-Koehler Publishers, Inc.
6   Kimmel, M. (2001) Masculinities and femininities. *International encyclopedia of the social and behavioral sciences.* Elsevier Science Ltd, 9318–9321.
7   Reeves, R. V. (2022) *Of Boys and men: Why the modern male is struggling, why it matters, and what to do about it.* The Brookings Institution.
8   Killingsworth, M. A. & Gilbert, D. T. (2010). A wandering mind is an unhappy mind. *Science 330* (6006) 932; DOI: 10.1126/science. 1192439.
9   Kabat-Zinn, J. (2009). *Wherever you go, there you are.* Adobe Digital Edition.

References

Adams, E. M. & Frauenheim, E. (2020) *Reinventing masculinity: The liberating power of compassion and connection.* Berrett-Koehler Publishers, Inc.

Cameron, C. D. (2017). Compassion collapse: Why we are numb to numbers. In E. M. Seppala et al. (eds) *The Oxford Handbook of Compassion Science.* Oxford University Press, pp. 262–271.

Connell, R. W. (1987). *Gender and power.* Stanford University Press.

Figley, C. R. & Figley, K. R. (2017). Compassion fatigue resilience. In E. M. Seppala et al. (eds). *The Oxford handbook of compassion science.* Oxford University Press, pp. 387–397.

Kabat-Zinn, J. (2009). *Wherever you go, there you are.* Adobe Digital Edition.

Killingsworth, M. A. & Gilbert, D. T. (2010). A wandering mind is an unhappy mind. *Science 330* (6006) 932. DOI: 10.1126/science. 1192439.

Kimmel, M. (2001) Masculinities and Femininities. *International Encyclopedia of the Social and Behavioral Sciences.* Elsevier Science Ltd, pp. 9318–9321.

Reeves, R. V. (2022) *Of Boys and men: Why the modern male is struggling, why it matters, and what to do about it.* The Brookings Institution.

9

YOUR PERSONAL JOURNEY OF COMPASSION

We hope you have enjoyed reading this book and found it informative, perhaps even inspirational. If so, we believe it can impact your life in a positive way.

We often talk about how focusing on compassion through our readings, practices, and writing this book has changed us over time. We both agree that compassion is a way of life, not a discrete practice or one-time action. We recommit ourselves daily to continuing our own journey. Doing so doesn't mean we never get irritable, angry, or do something we regret. Of course we do; we're only human and far from perfect. You'll remember that in the chapter on self-compassion, we talked about how the pursuit of personal perfection is an elusive quest. However, a compassionate mindset helps us realize this, accept our shortcomings, and just try to do our best. This mindset frames our lives by frequently getting us to reflect on this question: "What would compassion, as an orientation to living, lead us to do?" It helps us strive not only to practice compassion but to embody it. Yet, we recognize this journey takes time, and each day we strive to get better.

We also understand that mindfulness, the first of the seven virtues, is a daily practice and foundation for living a compassionate life. It's all too easy to get lost in everyday hassles, to fixate on what is wrong rather than what is right, to live in the past or the future, and to pay too much attention

DOI: 10.4324/9781003312437-12

to the small stuff. At some level, most daily hassles spring from small stuff, and a preoccupation with the more trivial matters of living diverts our attention from present-moment awareness. As the saying goes, "don't sweat the small stuff, it's all small stuff." Then, one day we wake up feeling as though life has passed us by. When we practice mindfulness each and every day, however, we wake up to the beauty of everything around us, like the smell of fresh air, the beauty of a flower blooming, or the wonder of the wind through the forest. We become open to new experiences in real time. We are reminded of this famous quote, often credited to Eleanor Roosevelt.

> Yesterday is history, tomorrow is a mystery and today is a gift: That's why they call it the present.

We also realize the importance of understanding what is beyond our control as well as what is within our control, meaning those issues, problems, or events we can take charge of. You may think that compassion is somewhat of a luxury, reserved for those whose lives are easy and calm. People who live under difficult conditions, however, want to get through each day, even just survive. Although difficult life circumstances are often outside of our control, how we respond to them is completely up to us, including what we attend to, what intention we set, and how we act.

Slowing down, meditating, and being mindful is easier when our lives are like a calm sea. When we encounter big waves, however, we can still practice mindfulness, leading to a life of compassion. In fact, we may need compassionate mindfulness even more to help us navigate these more challenging waters. Mindfulness and compassion can turn difficult situations into opportunities to build our self-confidence and to broaden and deepen our connections with others. Compassion helps us rise up in the face of tragedy and suffering.

As we have mentioned throughout this book, although we are "born to be good," we must learn to cultivate compassion and related virtues and practice applying compassion whenever we can, wherever we can, and as much as we can. Living a life of compassion truly is a symphony of the soul, where we are both conductor and musician. The symphony is our life—a large-scale composition we play with many different instruments. Hence, we must be skilled musicians. This requires learning and daily practice. We also must coordinate the different sections of our orchestra so we are in harmony with ourselves, others, and ultimately the planet. To do this, we must be skilled conductors, weaving together the different movements or acts of the complex music that is our life.

Your Personal Journey

So, are you ready to commit (or recommit) to forging a life of compassion? We hope so, because every person who makes this commitment not only adds to their own well-being, but to the well-being of others and the planet. You may think you're only one drop in a river, but a cascade of drops fills the river to its banks while flowing to fill the sea.

As we discussed in the "what" of compassion, especially its evolutionary basis, you came into this world prepared to do good, to orient your life to compassion. This sets you on a trajectory having multiple mental, emotional, behavioral, and relational benefits to enrich your life and the lives of others. It's a choice about how you want to live. It's truly up to you. Rest assured that you have what's needed to launch the journey.

As we've discussed, the first steps are to declutter your mind and surroundings to make room for peace, calm, comfort, and harmony. Decluttering is followed by focusing on the beauty within and around you and maintaining a positive orientation to how you relate to yourself and your world. Laying this foundation paves the way for setting your intention (making the commitment) to live a compassionate life.

Figure 9.1 We all must find our own path towards compassion.
Source: © Nancy Guerra and Kirk R. Williams

As we have stressed repeatedly, learning and living by contemplative practices will cultivate mindfulness in your life, which is the cornerstone of a compassionate life. Mindfulness will facilitate practicing the virtues of highly compassionate people as you climb the ladder of compassion. It will illuminate self-awareness so you can identify personal weaknesses to overcome and strengths to champion. Such awareness will fill your life with gratitude for who you are, what you have, and where you're going. Being open to expanding experiences in the world, based on self-confidence and personal agency, will enhance your skills at perspective taking and empathy. By maintaining this orientation, that is, climbing the ladder of compassion, you will find kindness toward yourself and others comes easier and easier, where you're willing to give of your personal gifts to help others.

This discussion is a very condensed summary of what we've talked about throughout the book. It may sound as though climbing the ladder of compassion is as easy as putting one foot in front of the other. For some, perhaps that's true, but for most of us, it's a challenging task. We're merely human, and as such, we'll backslide, make mistakes, and sometimes get exhausted along the way. We'll also run into circumstances that render living a compassionate life seemingly impossible, perhaps overcoming us from time to time. We all should expect challenges to happen along our journey, and when we stumble, avoid interpreting that experience as failure.

Figure 9.2 The beauty of a mountain lake in the Andes can soothe your soul.
Source: © Nancy Guerra and Kirk R. Williams

The important point is to accept that such challenges will happen and remain steadfast in our commitment (and recommitment) to living a life of compassion with all that it entails. As we've also stressed repeatedly, cultivating compassion is not a state to be achieved, an end product, or a destination. It's an orientation to living that involves a daily, disciplined practice, but one well worth doing.

Bon Voyage!

* * * *

We feel fortunate to have the opportunity to write this book and offer it to you. It's been an incredible shared experience. But then, even though we've had our challenges like most couples, we feel fortunate to have each other. After all, we can't just talk about gratitude, we must let it fill our lives.

Figure 9.3 The picture that doesn't need words.
Source: © Nancy Guerra and Kirk R. Williams

INDEX

Note: *Italic* page numbers indicate figures.

Printed in the United States
by Baker & Taylor Publisher Services